CAFFEINATE YOUR SOUL

52 Monday Mantras

ERICA GWYNN

www.mascotbooks.com

CAFFEINATE YOUR SOUL: 52 MONDAY MANTRAS

Cover image provided by Maryann Ligenza

For more information, please contact:
Mascot Books
620 Herndon Parkway #320
Herndon, VA 20170
info@mascotbooks.com

Library of Congress Control Number: 2019904769

CPSIA Code: PRV0220A
ISBN-13: 978-1-64307-519-8

Printed in the United States

To Olivia Grace

May you blossom into the beautiful, strong, faithful
warrior that God made you to be, and may you never
be afraid to shine your light.

Hi! I'm so happy and humbled and honored that you picked up this book. If we were in a coffee shop together, I'd ask you how you're doing—how you're *really* doing. And I'd want to know your honest answer. Not that automated, surface-level talk we quip back at cashiers or acquaintances. I mean really—how are you doing? Are you happy? Are you depressed? Are you hungry for some chicken fried rice, or hungry for more in your job? Are you struggling with your faith? Are you feeling really fulfilled in your friend group? Are you overwhelmed because it's Monday? Are you disappointed in someone—maybe in yourself? Are you looking for more in life?

Pour something hot 'n caffeinated into your mug of choice—it's high time we got better acquainted.

I'm Erica—a high-on-life wife, NICU mom, business owner, optimistic realist, and overachiever since birth. Ambivert, cat lady, ENFJ, and Enneagram Type 3.

Believer in red wine, bold lipstick, combat boots, and Jesus Christ.

I launched my business from my tiny, overcrowded college dorm room; I was at my dream school on a near-full financial aid scholarship, so everyone and their mom thought I must be Britney Spears-circa-2007 crazy to constantly put my entrepreneurial ambitions above corporate finance lectures. But I just knew in my gut that I wasn't put on this earth to push papers or crunch numbers. If you were—that's AWESOME. It was just clearly not my calling. But since I always loved to string words together and make people laugh or think twice, I figured forgoing economic policy would be a worthwhile swap for a few extra hours of writing. I'm also a bit of a personal development junkie. I love me my self-help like some folks love Diet Coke—it's a fix. God helps those who help themselves. I firmly believe that I can do all things through Christ who strengthens me—not Christ who comes down with a lightning bolt to zap earthly problems away like the plague. And I believe you can do all things with some strength, too. Whether your strength comes from Christ too, or from your therapist, your dad's dinner table talk, or your Nana's meatballs, my prayer is that you soon feel equipped and energized with a solid dose of perspective.

This book is made up of all of the advice I collectively lived by in my 20s that I think will best pave the path for my 30s, 40s and beyond (and yours, too). It's the good stuff from long talks with my mom (a.k.a., the best), or one-liners from my nana. It's everything I've shared with girlfriends over the years, or that girlfriends have shared with me in those moments when you might need it more than you want it.

But ask any of my girls and I think they'd agree—I'm not one for BS. I'm not one to fluff feathers with bull-crap to make you feel good now, if it won't make you feel better later, too.

So, I hope this book feels like coffee with a girlfriend who cares so much about you, she'll give it to you straighter than your shot of espresso on a Monday. *Caffeinate Your Soul* has got 52 Mantras inside — one for every Monday of the year. To get the most from this book (and to not feel completely overwhelmed), I recommend reading it in bite-size bits as written, one Monday at a time. Then, when you're done reading, let it hang out on your own coffee table at home for your girlfriends to sip on, too.

IF NOT NOW, WHEN?

And so begins a year's worth of Mondays.

Pours more coffee.

Come New Year's, everyone and their mom is swearing off carbs or committing to cardio. It's Resolution Station, and we're all hopping on that bandwagon. This is GREAT, but only for those things that made it onto the wagon.

What about those things that didn't make the annual Goals List…not because we don't want them to happen, but because we don't think they CAN?

The dreams that felt too big to dream.

…you know the ones.

The dreams that take a LOT to get there. The ones you might even keep secret, like writing a book, or starting a business. They feel immense. Gargantuan. Maybe possibly too big to chew in one piece, or in one year's worth of resolutions.

Or maybe the dreams that feel silly to be labeled as such, but you know would have SUCH positive impact on your everyday, like drinking half your body weight in H_2O, or carving out the first hour of every day to be all about prayer and gratitude.

And to those I say…

"If not now, when?"

Every single day—heck, every single second—is an opportunity to just do the damn thing already.

Our days are filled with choices. The average adult supposedly makes around 35,000 choices every day—35,000. Some are simple and relatively mindless in nature (brush your teeth, go to the bathroom, grab a salad for lunch, etc). And others might feel a bit more significant (break up with your boyfriend, quit your job, move across the country, etc). Every day, we have approximately 35,000 choices to make, and our days progress (or regress) accordingly. Choose to start that manuscript we've been dying to pen—progress. Choose to smoke another cigarette—regress. Choose to organize the kitchen cabinets—progress. Choose to yell at our neighbor about his dog—regress. The choices go on. As we choose our own paths, the question remains…

"If not now, when?"

Life is short; it's got no guarantees. Beyond this very moment, you have really no clue what comes next, if anything. Something could literally fall down from the sky right now and kill us all, and we'd be at the end of our story. So…why wait?

Why are you waiting to wear that dress that makes ya feel like a million?

Why are you waiting to use the good china?

Why are you waiting to try your expensive makeup?

Oftentimes, we "save" the best in our lives for a "special occasion," forgetting that life itself IS the special occasion. We've been awarded this life, and we have no actual idea how long we'll get to enjoy it.

…Chew on that for a hot sec. Think of how much more joy you'd be creating in your everyday life if you chose to view each day as a special occasion—each moment of NOW as your WHEN.

When will I start training for that half marathon? Now. Off to the gym.

When will I stop drinking a Diet Coke every single day? Now. No more Cokes in the grocery cart.

When will I take pride in my appearance, so that I feel GOOD whenever I look in the mirror? Now. Whatever that means—adding a little lipstick, changing out of pajama pants, brushing my hair, losing five pounds—starts now.

Not sure about you, but I for one do NOT want a bunch of woulda/coulda/shoulda running through my brain on my deathbed. Are you your best self right now? No? What's separating you from being that best self?

To test myself, I did the following lil' exercise: I started jotting down quick phone notes on my own best self. Turns out, a lot of 'em are tiny little tweaks that I could TOTALLY make every day, if only I'm intentional about it. Example: pumping myself up with my favorite jams on Spotify. Y'all, I lovelovelove music. I mean, I've been playing piano since age five, singing since shortly thereafter, am a musical theater junkie, and have upbeat pop music coursing through my veins. You'd think I'd at least have coffee shop acoustic on play in the background, but too often I catch myself in total silence. Why? Who the heck knows.

I'm also my best self when I actually style an outfit for the day instead of lazily throwing on jeans and a top. WHAT? You don't feel like a badass in your third day messy bun and oversized, spit-up-covered t-shirt? WHO KNEW? Friends, how EASY is it in the grand scheme of things to play music? Or to take two extra minutes to TRY in your closet instead of haphazardly grabbing something with an elastic waistband? Or to do whatever your thing is that would allow you to elevate just enough to get closer to that best self?

Fast forward five years—are you who you'd imagine you'd be?

Is your life full of good routines, or bad habits?

SO MANY QUESTIONS, I know. But really…if not now, when? We can push everything off to the hypothetical future that may or may not ever come—or we can take ownership of our lives. We can be the captains of our own ships, and we can put one foot in front of the other with intention, or we put on our metaphorical blindfolds and walk through life in the hopes of still stumbling upon our dream path.

So this week (and beyond), I challenge you, friends.

I challenge you to make it happen— whatever IT is—and to make it happen now. Someday isn't a good day. Tomorrow might never come. But today—right now— is what you've got. Make something of it.

I WILL STEP OUT

Girlfriend, we're in the new year. Too often, we wait for a 12,000 pound crystal ball drop to give us permission to start anew. It's like our goals and dreams are on hold until January 1...and then we go balls to the wall, full steam ahead doing #AllTheThings all at once until we inevitably burn out around Valentine's Day. What ends up happening isn't good. We become overwhelmed, and then we become paralyzed.

There are so many friggin' things on our lists of goals and resolutions that it can become too overwhelming and anxiety-inducing to even fathom. We freak out. We thought we did okay in setting some goals, but we failed to articulate how exactly we'll get there.

A few months (heck, maybe a few weeks) after "Auld Lang Syne" and we're back to bad habits and too-familiar routines, vowing to "try again next year."

Ugh. It feels crappy, doesn't it?

But it doesn't have to be so big—this huge, daunting thing that drops down into our laps as the ball drops into the new year.

I will step out.

As the saying goes, the journey of a thousand miles starts with the first step. New Year's resolutions are oh-so-hard and fail so often because they are too many miles without a map—too many lofty dreams and generic goals without broken down, specific points to get there.

If you're training for a marathon, you'd be stupid to just up and run 26 miles the day of the race. Sure, there's that sliver of possibility that somehow you pull through and manage to finish. Realistically, though, you can't just up and run 26 miles without training beforehand. I mean, I'd probably end up tripping over my own two feet and running down the block for a pizza instead...that is, if I didn't collapse first. In running a marathon, you'd be silly to start the race already worrying about the last mile, because you've got a whoooooole heckuvah lotta miles to get through before tackling the final sprint. And you'd be silly to jump right in without proper preparation, lest you fall flat on your face in pain. You've gotta go step by step—one at a time—with intention, action, commitment, and consistency. Whether you're just beginning training or you're starting the race itself, it all starts with one step. Then you take another step, and another, until finally, you've got a medal on your wall and the chance to do it all over again.

We fail the moment we want the medal without doing the work. But the work doesn't have to be difficult—it just has to be done.

Step out. I will step out.

Take the first step—or the next step. Step out of your comfort zone. Step out of your fear, step out of your inaction, nervousness, uncertainty, and excuses.

Actively, deliberately, intentionally take that step—whichever step needs taking—and then do not stop.

Ain't nobody got time for passive stepping. Passive stepping is literally not a thing. It is simply impossible to wait around for the new year, the next ball drop of life, expecting things to change just because the universe is moving forward. The world will keep spinning with or without you—wouldn't you rather take charge of your life and your direction, to step out and onto your own path of awesome?

I will step out.

There is nothing wrong with the old you—and there is no need for a whole "new you," either.

There IS something wrong with thinking things will just work in your favor and success will come as you sit idly hoping and wishing for it. That just ain't how it works, sis.

Take the reins, hoist up your ship's sails, sit in the driver's seat, put both hands on the wheel, and GO. Instead of vowing to do everything under the sun all at once right now because the calendar told you to, vow to strategically step out, one step at a time. Vow to step out no matter how scary or huge it might seem. Vow to KEEP stepping out regardless of what happens, because progress is only made through action. 365 days is a lot longer and harder than 24 hours. Start small, rinse, and repeat.

IT GETS better

IT GETS BETTER

Ah, Monday. Mondays got a bad rap. It's that day name that's always accompanied by an "UGH" or a sigh of dread. Everyone just waits in eager anticipation for any other day besides Monday, because any other day feels better than Mondaying does in that moment.

On Mondays, we can say, "*It gets better.*"

But sometimes life is harder than Mondays. Like, a *lot* harder. Real life has real sh*t, and when sh*t happens, sometimes we just need some semblance—ANY semblance—of hope to hold onto to remind us that maybe, just maybe, *it gets better.*

Because it's foolish to say that hands down, without a doubt, no fail, guaranteed it gets better. Do we *reaaally* know if "it" will get better?

Not really—not technically. Guarantees in life are few and far between, so I'm not about to step up onto a lofty soapbox to say that no matter what you're facing, regardless

of what you're experiencing, it will definitely get better.

But by the same token, we don't *really* know if it WON'T get better. Our luck and fate and direction can change at literally any given moment for so many different reasons, and we just cannot fathom the bigger picture of our lives (that's a job for only the Big Man Upstairs). It takes trust, it takes faith, it takes courage—and it takes hope. Sometimes, the only thing we can reasonably and realistically hold onto is the hope that it gets better.

It will, in time, get better.

Key #1: Don't define "it." It could be IT—the problem you're facing, the mountain you're climbing, etc. But IT could also be your strength, your adaptability, your tenacity, your problem-solving skills, your communication skills, or your creative thinking skills. It might feel like you're at the bottom of a hole with no way out or up, and there just might be no worse feeling than that of hitting rock bottom.

But sometimes, we need rock bottom.

We need rock bottom for perspective and appreciation when we're at the top.

We need rock bottom as a kick in the ass (when applicable) to get back on track.

We need rock bottom to remind us of how strong we really are.

And when we hit rock bottom, we need to remind ourselves that it gets better.

Because just when you think it can't, it can; just when you think it won't, it will.

Key #2: Never lose hope. Before this starts sounding like a cheesy Hallmark Christmas classic, let's just say it's not that. The whole point is to acknowledge that hope really IS an essential ingredient to staying as positive as possible in even the most desperate or discouraging times.

Ever see *The Shawshank Redemption?* It's such a good, classic movie (you MUST see), with hope as a central theme. This quote *pretty* much sums up the whole shebang:

"Hope is a good thing, maybe the best of things, and no good thing ever dies."

No matter what you're experiencing in your life right now girlfriend, I hope you feel encouraged and hopeful knowing that it gets better. It might get worse before it gets better, and it might not get better for a long time. But, *it gets better.*

Remember it, hold on to it, never forget it.

"We need rock bottom for perspective and appreciation when we're at the top. We need rock bottom as a kick in the ass (when applicable) to get back on track. We need rock bottom to remind us of how strong we really are. And when we hit rock bottom, we need to remind ourselves that it gets better. Because just when you think it can't, it can; just when you think it won't, it will."

#CAFFEINATEYOURSOUL

i am stronger now

I AM STRONGER NOW

Our first baby was born two months early, totally unexpectedly. About 30 weeks into my pregnancy, things started going downhill, and my due date became a "delivery date" which kept inching forward with each passing day, for both her and my safety. All we knew was that she had been "measuring small," and I had been diagnosed with severe pre-eclampsia. Two months from my due date, after a lengthy, nerve-wracking ultrasound, my doctor came in the room to deliver the news:

"You are much sicker than you feel. Right now, you're at high risk of seizure, stroke, or both. We have to take the baby out, for both of your safety."

"Okay. . .when?"

"Today. As soon as an operating table opens up."

I had an emergency C-section that day, and my beautiful Olivia was born at 2:34 p.m. weighing all of three pounds. The journey from there was the hardest of my life so far. For the next 73 days, she was in the NICU. 73 days. Where most mamas bring their babies home after two or three days, mine lay in an incubator in a hospital for two and a half months. Not only that, but she had been transferred halfway into her NICU stay from the hospital she was born at, five minutes from our house, to the greatest children's hospital in the world—an hour and a half away. I battled postpartum depression. I battled crippling anxiety. I battled so much exhaustion from traveling to spend as much time as allowed by her bedside. I battled so much pain being separated from my baby, not knowing when she would be okay (and sometimes, not knowing IF she would be okay). When I shared my struggle on social media, I was met with SO much love, and so many folks saying that my "strength" had inspired them.

Hold up—strength?

I was showing up on my Instagram

Stories in tears, just giving what little updates I could so that my followers didn't think that I had died—literally. I didn't want to talk; I didn't know what to say—I just showed up to ask for prayers because it was the only thing I KNEW we needed in such uncharted territory. I admitted feeling ANYTHING but strong. I felt depressed and weak and sad and drained and in so much pain that some days I would just sit on the floor and sob, crying out to God to please take away the cup. To take away HER cup—let me drink it if I could, if it would mean she could come home and just be okay. To make it through and be strong. Other days I would just feel completely empty, devoid of any emotion at all. A zombie just moving from one place to the next, words just bouncing off of my shell.

I didn't feel strong. But you know what? I was.

The collective crowd of women reading this is a dang strong group, of that I am sure. YOU are strong.

Of the group reading these words right now alongside you, someone has been through chemotherapy. Someone has been bullied. Someone has been raped. Someone has been addicted to prescription drugs, and someone has been on the receiving end of racism. Someone has been told she's "too fat" or "too dumb" or "too much" of something for someone else.

Are you that someone?

Everyone is someone who has been through something, and yet, we have all survived. If you are sitting here on this Monday, book in hand with maybe a really good cappuccino or Cabernet—you've made it.

You are so strong.

I know you are stronger now.

You might feel the farthest thing from "strong," but you are stronger now for having been through all of the sh*t you've been through. If you were to flashback to before and ask younger you if she thought she could do it, she might've said no. She might've thought there was NO WAY JOSE that she'd get to the other side of whatever mountain was about to appear in the landscape ahead.

But she did it. YOU did it.

Kanye said it best: "That that don't kill me can only make me stronger." Even if you're in the midst of your mountain right now, you are stronger now for having begun the climb. Your muscles are being worked, but muscles only get stronger the more they're flexed.

Your strength is being flexed right now, sister. You are stronger now for continuing the climb.

If your mountain is already in the rearview mirror, give yourself a pat on the back, girlfriend. Say it with me, "I am stronger now." You're still standing, and you're stronger now than yesterday—like Britney Spears coming out of 2007.

Keep going. Keep believing. Keep hoping. Keep praying. Just keep swimming. You are stronger now.

Word on the statistics street is that 80 percent of folks fail at New Year's resolutions by the end of January, and most others give it up come mid-February.

Dude.

Those are some friggin' depressing statistics!

Are you part of the 80 percent? Or are you part of the 20 percent still going strong? (I'm about half and half on my own list!) Everyone vows "New year, new me!" and tries to change their whole entire life overnight (literally). That is SO. MUCH. PRESSURE to make so much happen, when psychologically, that's just not a setup for success! Science says it takes 30 days to form a new habit—so how on God's green earth can you expect to totally overturn not just one, but every single bad habit in your life from December 31st to January 1st—a 24-hour turnaround time? From working out to drinking water to saving money to reading more, it's like wham bam alakazam—new life alert! I mean, PROPS girlfriend…it's ambitious AF.

But it's also discouraging AF if/when you slip up, which I think is to blame for that alarmingly high failure rate come January 31st.

Beyond that, why wait until the new year to finally make those very important strides towards our best self? We know we should, we think we could…so why would we wait until a shiny ball drops in a crowded square to start doing the things we should/could/would be doing already, if only we CHOSE to do so?

I've always had beef with the whole "new year, new me" mantra.

So I made a new one. Enter: new day, new me.

Today is a new day. Today is a new day!

You have just as much power to do something different today as you did at 11:59 p.m. on December 31st. How amped up were you at the end of the year to write a list and check it twice, of dreams and plans and goals and changes for the "best year ever?"

You were pretty darn amped.

You were ready. You were hopeful. You were committed. Then, life happened. For whatever reason, you fell off the wagon. Maybe you just stumbled a little, almost fell, but are still on it. Or maybe, you fell off so hard, you've got emotional bruises from the fall. Either way, it's okay.

No, it's not okay to quit—to give up on yourself. But it IS OKAY to admit temporary defeat, and get back on the saddle stronger, smarter, better. To acknowledge a mistake or a flub up, choose a new direction, and head there with commitment.

Today. Right now.

Because a new you doesn't have to wait for a new year—a new you can begin today. New day, new me.

It might feel easy to strive for more gym time or less potato chips to kick off the new year strong on paper, if those aren't particularly scary or even truly challenging goals for ya—or, if they're not the most meaningful. You jot 'em down, you make it a few weeks, and then you aren't TOO mad if/when you slip into old habits. But when you can't commit to the "easy" goals on your list, how the heck are you supposed to stick with harder, longer, bigger, better goals?

Making a champagne-fueled commitment at midnight for the next 365 days is a tall order, girlfriend. The second the sparkles disappear, though, we're faced with the sameness and the habits that kept us feeling a certain way and doing certain things for the LAST 365 days.

Wanna up that success rate? To get out of the 80 percent and into the top 20?

Forget the year.

"The journey of a thousand miles begins with one step." It's one of my favorite quotes, from an ancient Chinese philosopher, Lao Tzu. It's important here, because you know what a year is made up of?

Days. 365 of 'em. New day, new me. The yearlong journey of 365 days still begins with just one.

Wake up every single day with a new resolve to hit the treadmill, read your Bible, put down the Diet Coke, learn to speak Spanish. When you can look ahead and actually see the finish line, you're more likely to sprint to make it happen. It feels reachable and doable. Because it is.

While it's still reachable and doable with a zoomed-out lens, it's not in your immediate view, so motivation may falter. You might get comfy in your pace, slow down, or stop altogether. It's like running a marathon versus running a 100-meter sprint. You might not even get your butt off the couch to begin training for a marathon if it feels just so totally overwhelming. Running 100 meters, on the other hand, is (only) one-fourth of a track. You can totally do that. Then, you can do it again, and again, and eventually you realize you can run and you can keep running until you work up to the big kahuna.

A year is just 365 days. Who's to say it has to start on January 1st?

Your year starts now, with this day. New day, new me. Make it happen, and make it count.

I AM WORTHY OF LOVE

When V-Day is right around the corner, it's hard to escape the hearts-fest that throws up on every store end cap—from pink balloons to red roses to pink AND red candies and chocolates galore, the season of St. Valentine shows the heck up. This time of year can be particularly meh for any of us not feelin' the love in some aspect of life, be that romantically, with our girlfriends, or with ourselves. When we're not feelin' it, it can be far too easy to equate a lack of momentary feeling to a lack of permanent worth. We doubt we're worth the "perfect guy," we doubt we're worth the ultimate girl squad...we doubt our own worth point blank period, letting our self-love slip in the process.

Listen, we've all been through sh*t in life at some point or another.

We've been bullied.

We've been dumped.

We've been intentionally excluded.

We've also been the one doing the bullying or dumping or excluding sometimes, because we're human and imperfect and make mistakes and fall short.

But we're all worthy of love. No matter what you've been through, no matter what you've done, you are still—and always will be—worthy of love. In case you don't fully believe that yet in your heart of hearts, I need you to look in the nearest mirror right this very second and repeat after me:

"I AM WORTHY OF LOVE!!!"

I know right now you're probably chuckling, thinking E, you crazy! and not actually looking in the mirror and giving yourself the pep talk. Stop, and find a mirror! I need you to be your own damn hype squad right now, girlfriend. Represent. Show up. You are worthy of love. You are worth more than your fears. You are worth more than your self-doubts. You are worth more than the negative thoughts and vibes and things being thrown at you from seemingly every corner of the universe sometimes. You are worthy of a good life, a fulfilling life, and a life that makes you excited to wake up to every single morning. Regardless of what you feel right now in this moment, it would be so silly—oh so silly!—to let any momentary blip permanently mess with your self-love, self-worth, and willingness to spread love to other people.

"Now" never means "forever." Just because you don't have, feel, or think something now doesn't give it any sort of permanence in your life unless you let it.

"Feel" doesn't have to mean "am/are." Feeling is not being. Emotions do not define us. While your emotions are totally valid and totally okay to feel, that does not also automatically mean that what you feel accurately reflects what exists in real life.

- **Feeling ugly doesn't make you ugly.**

- **Feeling fat doesn't make you fat.**

- **Feeling stupid doesn't make you stupid.**

- **Feeling unworthy of love doesn't actually make you unworthy of love.**

What we feel so oftentimes is reflective of our now, and it can be really freaking HARD to separate the feeling from the being in more cases than we'd like to admit. We feel something now, and we jumble it together with "forever" and "being" instead of feeling. It can overwhelm us, because we can't identify what the heck we're even feeling sometimes, let alone what the reality of a situation is. Unfortunately, more often than not, we give ourselves the shortest end of the stick. We hardly give ourselves the grace that we often give others. We've heard the stories—people blatantly disrespecting and cheating on their partners and still getting second chances, third chances, fourth chances to "make it right." Yet, after one failed attempt of our own to do or try something new, we label ourselves "a failure" unworthy of future success or happiness.

Where the heck does the snowball start?! I swear the seemingly smallest thing could happen sometimes, stick with us subconsciously (whether we even realize it or not), and come back full force at a later date with more serious impact, causing us to question our very core. Suddenly we're lacking in self-love and abundant in self-loathing and our true worth isn't even in the scope of our understanding, because we can't even believe that we're worthy of the goodness in front of us.

How sad is that???

Some asshat at your job could call you incompetent—that doesn't make it true, or make you unworthy of love.

Some insecure girl could say you're just not going to get very far in life—that doesn't make it true, or make you unworthy of love.

Some jerk on a first date could tell you that he just doesn't see it going anywhere beyond the nightcap—that doesn't make it true, or make you unworthy of love.

Girlfriend, you are worth SO MUCH. You are awesome. God made you Himself. He specifically and strategically formed you in His hand, how He wanted you to be. Then He sent down His own son to die for you, because you're worth THAT MUCH to Him. You are worthy of love because He loves you, and that is enough.

i will carry on

You know those days when you just CANNOT?

Oh, I just can't with my boss—if she throws one more thing on my plate right now, I'm walking in on Friday and quitting.

I just can't with my children—if I hear "MOM!" one more time in the next 32 seconds, I'm changing my name.

Last Tuesday, I had approximately seven meltdowns by 2 p.m. So yeah, was doin' real well.

It was the hot mess express over at Coming Up Roses headquarters (aka, my kitchen table), and I was not on top of my game. *But in our lowest moments, that's when we are given the grace and strength to grow high again.*

Later that day, I had a call with one of my cohorts behind the blog scenes, and we were talking about a few challenges we were facing on the social media scene. I had gone into the call *so insanely frustrated* about a whole LOT of things. This algorithm cut my reach in half—it won't show my posts to people who have CHOSEN to follow me? How nutty is that? And that algorithm? It changed last week, and word on the social media street is it just changed AGAIN! If you're not ahead on the trend, you're behind, and it's confusing and exhausting and frustrating when any outreach for direct help from the source is met with radio silence. Totally specific to my own job, but maybe you've felt the same—your kid just WOULD. NOT. NAP. for anything and it threw off your *entire* mental game plan for the day, or you've ventured into a new class, and you cannot for the LIFE of you wrap your head around biochemistry. Or maybe, your boss just piled onto your workload, but the team is understaffed and you're out in deep water to get things done on deadline.

But we hung up and I felt *better.* Not fixed by any means, but better.

And better is, well, BETTER.

It got me thinking about a Q that I had been asked recently on overcoming obstacles and "battles" in life. I thought it was the LAST thing I should be writing about at that moment, since I was not at all feelin' like an overcomer or conqueror of *any* obstacle that day.

…Which is exactly why it needed to be conquered intentionally. Right now.

"I will carry on."

A simple statement with bold impact when decisively said.

I. Will. Carry. On.

Today's Monday Mantra is more than a mantra—it's a declaration. In our lowest lows, the LAST thing we feel like doing is declaring victory over something. Because we don't feel strong—we feel weak, sad, exhausted, the works. We don't feel victorious or brave or capable. We might feel blatantly defeated.

Which is exactly when and why we need to make a bold decision with bold impact to reverse the onslaught of negativity that is currently catapulting us into a downward spiral of bad feels.

Y'all, I am the QUEEN of spiraling.

Seriously. Queen Spiral, at your service. Whenever I'm in a rut (*just ask my husband*), I have this not-so-good tendency to go right to the worst-case scenario in my head. Soon, the Scale Three Situation is now rocketing past 10 and into SOS Emergency territory, for no good reason other than I allowed my brain to take it there. It's like when I was in college; scoring poorly on one test would turn into me thinking I was going to fail the class, fail the year, fail school completely, and lose all career aspirations, settling to working a drive-thru window for the rest of forever. *All because I did not-so-hot on one test.* I mean, sure, failing exams ain't optimal, but it's also no reason to whip out the nuclear codes and call code red. *Can ya relate?*

It's all in the mind, really.

It's all in the mind.

When we're facing any sort of obstacle or battle in life, how it affects us AND how we respond (versus react) are entirely dependent on how we THINK about the situation at hand. Because how that exact same obstacle would affect Nancy Next Door would depend on how *she* would think about it, etc.

How we think is such a unique experience, typically so deeply rooted in a thousand different past experiences, thoughts, and lessons. So how we approach challenges and how we mentally scale mountains before beginning the actual climb depends entirely on what's going on in our pretty little brains leading up to the point of action. The fears, worries, and anxieties that might try and work their way into your heart and head are different than those for our good friend Nancy Next Door because you're two entirely different people with entirely different *everything*. I know I'm guilty of sometimes trying to make myself feel better about a situation by looking at the neighbor's grass, so to speak, to see whose is greener. You too? We let our attitudes about a roadblock or obstacle be affected by how we think so-and-so is handling it, or how we "should" be reacting since so-and-so said "xyz." But that doesn't truly serve us—it might serve our ego temporarily, but it doesn't truly serve us in our growth towards our best selves.

I will carry on.

A phrase entirely dependent on YOUR attitude towards YOUR obstacles.

Not Nancy Next Door's, but yours.

I've seen way too many folks sadly fall prey to a victim mindset. They feel like everyone and their mom is out to get them; they're doing everything right and just not getting their way; life has handed them the shortest stick in the lot and it's JUST SO UNFAIR, yadda yadda yadda. *Feeling defeated because of the outside, while not elevating or adjusting on the inside.*

While it's oh so easy to think that we have no control, and to just surrender to the circumstances around us, it's oh so *important* to recognize that both of those ideas are false and unhelpful.

Sure, we're not always (or ever) in

complete control of what happens to us or around us. But we ARE in control of how we think. Because for any and every thought that comes through our head, we have the power to say yes or no—to allow it to hang out and be pondered, or to say NOPE SIR and move on to the next mental topic.

When I was "having a sh*t day" last week, I realized that I spent a casual four hours being completely unproductive, doing absolutely nothing. *I'm sorry…what?* Yup. By the time I was over the wallowing, I confronted myself. *Self, what did you do today? What did you DO to actively address the sh*t?*

And I had no good answer.

Because the truth was, I had done NOTHING. I had not carried on.

I had let myself stop and wallow in stagnancy. When my attitude was not action-oriented, it was just blah—and no good action could possibly come from it. My attitude had been depressed, half EXPECTING the next bad thing to happen on an assuredly bad day. So…what the heck could be expected to happen except *more bad things*? I certainly wasn't doing anything to bring about GOOD, so how could I expect a change?

It's all in the mind—a simple mindset shift with the power to direct our next step. *I will carry on.*

What altered the course of our phone call that day was a simple attitude adjustment. My friend and I went in feeling discouraged and disgruntled, like social media is out to get us. Algorithms won't let us win, everything is pay to play, *yadda yadda yadda, you know the drill.* Midway through the conversation, though, our negative tone shifted and we focused on action steps to move forward. Sure, we might not know what the HECK any one algorithm or the next is doing from one week to the next (or heck, from Tuesday to Wednesday), but we can do SOMETHING with what we DO know. We can either wallow in self-pity and throw the woe-is-me party (which is really un-fun for, well, everyone), or we can decide we'll friggin' CARRY. ON.

I won't dare say "keep calm" and carry on, because Lord only knows keeping calm has never been this girl's strongest suit. But we have the power to at least carry on with a next step. That next step can help us or hurt us—it depends entirely on the attitude with which we're steppin'.

I will carry on, and so can you.

Give yourself GRACE

GIVE YOURSELF GRACE

Hello, my name is Erica, and I'm a recovering perfectionist. You?

I'll skip the life story and head straight to its ugly manifestation in my day-to-day life—namely, the to-do list.

Oh, the to-do's. There's just SO MUCH TO DO, yo! As an entrepreneur since age 19, running a business with zero help whatsoever (*besides my mom hopping behind a camera shutter now and then—thanks, Mom!*), I became accustomed to having 32 and a half things on each day's list of to-do's, and I'd workworkwork until all 32 and a half things were done.

But, I was also addicted to the hustle. I was addicted to the oh-so-glorious feeling of crossing OFF to-do's. That sense of accomplishment. The rush! The thrill!

I'd work from sunup to sundown (no joke) without ceasing if it meant I crossed everything off of that dang list.

But what happened if/when I started missing a thing or two? I mean, it was inevitable. I am human. *We are human.* It is actually impossible to do it all *all* of the time. I wasn't magically making more time in a day, but I somehow expected the hours to grow alongside my ever-expanding list of dreams and goals.

I was giving myself NO grace. I started feeling underwhelmed by my daily routines—things that typically I lovelovelove and feel GRATEFUL for, if anything—and overwhelmed by all of the ideas and what-ifs and maybes that were filling my brain. Soon, it became a not-so-good pity party of one, feeling guilty for feeling badly and then feeling even *more* overwhelmed from the guilt on top of the tension, stress, and other random anxiety.

Ain't nobody got time.

Too often, we're just *too damn hard* on ourselves.

We need grace. You need grace. You need to give YOURSELF grace. The hardest thing for me to grapple with grace is its kryptonite: perfectionism.

Perfectionism kills grace.

Me being this overachieving, Type A perfectionist usually means that I'm the actual worst at giving myself grace. Or, I can give myself grace in the moment…but the unintended consequence means internalizing something as a failure instead of a grace-given moment. *No bueno.* I'll use past tense for the following since my therapist back in the day told me so. (*She always said to use the past tense since we have the ability to recreate and better ourselves every single moment and are not defined by our pasts—isn't that cool?! Thank you, Karen!*) If in the midst of being so caught up in my work, Jamie threw in a load of laundry or Swiffered the kitchen floor, I'd consider myself a crappy wife in that moment instead of giving myself grace and just appreciating the fact that I've got a bombdotcom husband. After a packed day of work projects, which often consists of hopping between my inbox and writing while shooting content or being on calls,

some messages may inevitably be missed. When that happens, I'd tell myself that I'm a terrible blogger, suck at my job, and don't deserve to be doing what I'm doing for a living.

Isn't that escalation just insane?

Looking back with clarity and hindsight, it seems like a no-brainer. Both are untrue statements in their respective scenarios, and both lead to unnecessary sadness, anxiety, and blatant depression if left untreated with graceful fingers. But in the moment, when it feels oh so real, it can be hella hard to keep level-headed and give ourselves *grace* instead of hammering down on why we're not *smarter, faster, prettier, better.*

I think we all face situations like that.

We fall short on something we think we shouldn't, and it turns into this bigger thing—this negative spiral of bad thoughts and blatant LIES that we tell ourselves in those moments. Then these, in turn, damage our self-worth, lessen our self-love, and keep us further from our best self.

Give yourself grace.

Let yourself mess up and make mistakes—*just learn from them.*

Let yourself feel bad—*just actively work on feeling better again.*

Let yourself fall down—*just get back up.*

Whether it's a momentary setback or blah time (just feelin' funky on a given Tuesday, etc), or a bigger, more unchangeable roadblock (a death of someone close to you, etc), give yourself grace to get through it in its due time. Don't let feelings change the facts of who you are, Whose you are, and the inherent worth you have as a beautiful, blessed, BOSS human being.

Understand that *while it might not always feel like it when scrolling your Instagram feed*, nobody's perfect. Seriously.

Know that you're not alone. Ever.

Trust that everything happens for a reason, and your reason might not be known, comfortable, easy, and/or all of the above right now (slash ever).

At the end of the day, the King of Kings gives grace to you and me endlessly, day after day and time after time. We don't deserve it—He does it because of who HE is and not who WE are. So if He can give you grace…you can (and should) give yourself grace, too.

Grace is longer than the rest of your to-do list and taller than your Starbucks order on the middle of a Wednesday.

Grace is enough.

Give yourself grace.

ENLARGE Your Territory

ENLARGE YOUR TERRITORY

Ever been to a weekend-long retreat or conference? You know, the ones that get you HYPED, rock your world, and change your life in the span of 48–72 hours?

Yup, I lovelovelove me the conference life.

Not too long ago, I spent the weekend at a faith retreat, and I *truly* felt like a new woman heading into the week. God worked some *wonders* in my life, and I found myself just sitting there with my Honey Nut Cheerios like GOD IS SO STINKIN' GOOD HALLELUJAH.

One of the strongest stories stuck with me long after the Bibles closed.

Enlarge your territory.

This all stemmed from the idea of cleaning our nets. *What the heck does that mean, E?*

Let's get biblical for a hot sec, shall we?

In the Bible, there's a story about the disciples fishing (Luke 5, FYI). They're goin' at it all night, to no avail. Jesus happens upon them when they're back at shore, cleaning their nets. He told them to put their nets into the deep water for a catch. Simon Peter says, "Master, we worked hard all night and caught nothing, but I will do as You say and let down the nets." He trusts, he throws his net on the other side of the boat as Jesus tells him to…and he ends up with so much fish, his nets break and he needs help to bring it all back to shore! *Pause.*

From even just a historical standpoint, put yourself in these guys' shoes.

For many back in this day, fishing wasn't just a hobby to do with dad on a hot summer weekend—it was a livelihood. Not catching any fish wasn't just a bummer—it could've been a *big* bummer, because it was kinda sorta like totally failing at your job. Like you're a salesperson who didn't make a single sale, or a baker with zero cake orders. So imagine how you feel if/when you just blatantly *fail* at your job.

…It sucks, doesn't it?

If/when you do fail, you're probably not

still jumping up and down ready to go try again—you probably end up feeling kinda *sucky* and ready to call it a day, toss in the towel (or net), and quit altogether.

That's how these dudes were feeling, and then here comes Jesus saying, "Just put the net on the other side!"

Simple enough, right?

I feel like if that were me, I would've been *pissed.*

Like, really? *You don't think I haven't tried that already, Lord? I've been working my tail off all night doing my job—you don't think I haven't tried different angles, or different waters, or different nets by now? I've tried, I've fallen short. I'm donezo.*

BUT WAIT. We need to enlarge our territory.

When we try without trusting, we're not truly trying—we're testing.

We're entering a situation with doubt or fear, and that inevitably impacts the final result whether we realize it at the time or not. Sometimes we get so caught up in our routine or in our day-to-day life that we blatantly FORGET to keep options truly open. We go through the motions, we do what we *think* we're supposed to do (or heck, even what we know we're supposed to do to at least just get the job done), and we expect results to be per usual. Then when they're not, we stop. We quit. We call it a day. We start to shrink instead of leaning in and expanding more.

We close off our territory, so to speak. We get routinized. We get comfortable.

But that's not what God wants for us, and it's not what will bring about our best selves or our most abundant lives.

Even if you're not a believer, ain't nobody got time for being close-minded or thinking small! You were made for more. You were made for more than you THINK you were made for, and you won't discover that until you take the next step and enlarge your territory. Being the biggest fish in a small pond doesn't make you the biggest fish—it's just indicative of your perspective at that given moment in that given space. So no matter where you are in life, chances are you have room to expand. You've got space to grow, area to maximize, territory to explore, whether that's in the number of fish you catch, lipsticks you sell, or the number of people you pass in your everyday life whose lives you could make a little brighter, a little kinder, with a smile.

Nothing good ever grows in comfort zones. It's like this awesome combo of getting a little uncomfortable and trusting God and then BOOM. It happens. We enlarge our territory. We grow. We gain. We have more to give. Just like in Luke 5.

It's time to think bigger.

It's time to stop playing small.

REFUSE to play small.

Refuse to get too comfortable that you fail to see the opportunity ahead. We have no real clue what's truly in store for us; none of us do. Heck, you can think you're at the end of your rope—and all logical signs might point to that, too—and then one thing comes along to shake it up and change the game. The second you start to feel comfortable is the second you need

to step it up, enlarge your territory, and GROW.

Step out on that limb. Go the extra distance. If you feel a gentle nudge from somewhere in the universe to try something new, be like Simon Peter and Nike and JUST DO IT. You might just find your nets too full to function, in all the best ways.

CUT the NOISE

I've got a love/hate relationship with New York City.

Have you been?

Don't get me wrong—New York is magical. There's just something about street pretzels and the smell of pee in the subways that gets millions of folks totally JAZZED to make their dreams happen, and if that's not magic at work I don't know what is.

It's the City that Never Sleeps, and it's never without its noise. In actuality, NYC is not alone in the din—this is a noisy world in which we live. The bustling city of hustlers, the bustling *home* of hustlers, bustling families, bustling internets—everything is bustling, everything is saturated, everything is go-go-go. Cars honking, babies crying, people yelling, *noise, noise, noise.*

Beyond the literal noise of it all, there's the noise that comes from just too much happening too much of the time: content coming at us from every direction, choices to make at every turn, distractions available wherever we look. *Noise, noise, noise.* Sometimes, *it's just too much.*

In my own life, noise almost *always* leads straight to Burn Out Station. If/when I let too much random noise creep into my life, I lose focus. I lose confidence. I lose a sense of direction, because I'm trying to let the noise of society guide my path instead of God (whoa now, deep). Since noise can be envisioned as a literal swirling sea of rubbish overhead...that's a WHOLE lot less effective a guide than, *oh I dunno*, the One who created it all in the first place.

Cut the noise.

Put on your blinders (and earplugs), girlfriend.

Cut the noise. Be willing and able to ignore the swimming sea of *everything* that's constantly encircling your head to focus solely on what actually matters in your life. Prioritize the things that matter, the tasks that matter, the people that matter—and cut the rest.

Drop 'em like flies in your mind, because at the end of the day, they literally don't matter.

It might sound harsh, but it's a lot harsher on *yourself* to put an expectation there that you're going to do all the things for all the people, all the time. You won't do it all—you can't. None of us can. You'll just find yourself overwhelmed, overworked, and over it all in the end, right back at good ol' Burn Out Station.

Cut the noise before it becomes too loud.

This can be so much easier said than done, I know. I know because as someone who usually cares way too much about way too many things, I sometimes need constant reminders from my inner circle about what truly matters, and what doesn't.

That coworker who keeps giving you side-eye because you got promoted before them? *Cut the noise.* Their insecurity is not a reflection of you; it's a reflection of THEM.

That random chick who keeps subtweeting you? *Cut the noise.* (Social media is exhibit A for this phenomenon.) Until she musters up the chutzpah to have an *actual* conversation with you, her passive aggression is completely irrelevant, immature BS not worth a second of your digital breath.

That guy you met on Tinder who you actually really liked, but who's now stringing you along because he wants to play the field and "keep things open"...and you not-so-secretly actually want a real relationship? *Cut the noise.* You only live once, in the least cliché way possible. You can be on different pages with different people for different reasons, but when it comes to love, find someone who is on—or who can GET on—your same page lickety-split.

That family member who keeps giving you you-know-what for deciding that you actually don't want to use your biochemistry degree in a lab, but rather want to make your dream of owning your own clothing boutique happen? *Cut the noise.* Your life is yours and yours alone. If they want to get a biochemistry degree and don a lab coat, they can. Until then, you're the only one whose head hits your pillow at night, and you need peace with your own decisions to sleep soundly. Everyone and their mother has an opinion—not all of them matter to you.

When we fail to hit a goal, chances are it was partly because we let too much noise cloud our process. This is almost *always* a piece of my own puzzle if I fall short on something. Whenever I get sidetracked, start multitasking, or fail to plan…I'm basically planning to fail. When the noise of the world creeps into my space, I lose clarity and focus and can't necessarily stop it. So in comes the noise, and out goes any chance of staying on track to make it happen. *Womp.*

To cut out the noise and stay on track, it comes down to the breakdown of NEED versus WANT, and acting accordingly.

First and foremost, what do you NEED to achieve? What's GOTTA happen no matter what for normal life to proceed on schedule?

Do that.

Second thing's second: What do you WANT to achieve? What's on that list of, "*If I have time, I'd lovelovelove to do _____?*"

Do that.

For me, my goal is to wake up and first read my devotionals and Bible app—NOT all of my social media. I need to cut out the noise of blinking red social media notifications to focus on what I actually need to do: prioritize my faith. If I have time after, *then* I can scroll Instagram, but if and only if I've done the "need" first. Capiche?

When we become too consumed with what other people think of us, we're letting the noise of the world overpower the noise of our own hearts, or the peace from knowing what the One who really matters thinks of us.

To cut out the noise and feel peace in relationships, we must recognize which relationships are actual *relationships* that matter in the grand scheme of things…versus which "relationships" are just a connection that social media says is so. Remember that not all Facebook friends are created equal—we aren't obligated to treat them as so, either. If someone you barely know is expecting an inappropriate amount of your time or energy just because it would benefit them in some way, you aren't obligated to give it. You're allowed to say no.

Which relationships NEED nurturing, because they're the most important in your life?

Your immediate family, your best friends, your grandparents? Nurture those that mean the most to you.

Then, which relationships do you WANT to nurture, because they're important and you want them to stay on good course?

Other great friends, those good souls you meet along the way...etc.

Someone can get in your face or space for whatever reason, expecting a piece of you. They are noise; it's up to you how to adjust the volume in your head.

"It might sound harsh, but it's a lot harsher on yourself to put an expectation there that you're going to do all the things for all the people, all the time. You won't do it all—you can't. None of us can. Cut the noise before it becomes too loud."

#CAFFEINATEYOURSOUL

WHY THE HELL NOT?

WHY THE HELL NOT?

It's what you say when you're faced with a choice—an adventure worth taking.

It's what you say when you sense an upside, and aren't too sure of any downsides.

It's also what you say when your husband whips out the Grey Goose or the Ben & Jerry's on a Tuesday after the kids are tucked in bed.

It's a declaration of fearlessness, and a vow to live life fully in spite of fear-driven what-ifs. A vow to make it happen. Because *why the hell not?*

Our lives can be full of joy, intention, ambition, and action, or our lives can be full of disappointment, regret, carelessness, and fear. One of those sets is a whole heck-uvah lot more fulfilling than the other. The difference in the outward manifestation of our goals, dreams, and desires often comes with the seemingly simplest of mindset shifts.

The haves have one thing that the have-nots do not have, and it's all in the mind.

To do truly great things in life, we have to be willing to take truly great risks. Everyone's idea of "risk" is different—some might think of investing a large sum of cash, while others think of interpersonal relationships or a cross-country move. We all have risks to take, and we all have fears to face. It's no coincidence that our definition of "risk" is oftentimes most closely correlated to our definition of "fear."

But fear is all in our head.

The odds of certain outcomes get all skewed when fear takes hold, and the "risk" either grows or shrinks based on whether we control our fears or they control us. *Why the hell not?* is a mantra often maintained only by those with a little bitta booze in their system, because it encourages this idea of fearlessness…which oftentimes, unfortunately, is only brought about by some substance or another. Which is so sad, because we are destined to be so much more than that!

When you're facing a fear, you can think of 32 reasons why it's a bad idea to attempt xyz.

Speak in public? You'll probably vomit in front of a room of people if you dare open your mouth.

Talk to that cute guy at work? He'll totally laugh in your face, or he just won't even acknowledge your presence and you'll just be standing there awkwardly wanting to disappear.

Start a blog? You have no clue what you're doing, other people are already doing it better, you don't "have the time," and you don't know if people will like it.

But let's take fear out of the above pictures.

Speak in public? *Why the hell not?* Sure, maybe you'll flub up a word or two. You're scared of looking silly to others, but a LOT of people share your pain and aren't the biggest fans of public speaking. You might not be perfect, but nobody is. You have something important to say, and speaking in public might mean that somebody who needs to hear your message hears you when they otherwise wouldn't. Plus, you'll feel amazing afterwards, for either proving yourself wrong and knocking it outta the park, or for simply *getting it done* (or both!).

Talk to that cute guy? *Why the hell not?* Sure, maybe he won't show interest back. You're scared of feeling unwanted or uninteresting, but a LOT of people share your pain and aren't the biggest fans of making the first move when they already feel vulnerable. But when you have an opportunity to connect with someone, how they respond is not in your control (ever). Fate may allow some things to happen, but fate can't make much happen if we lock ourselves up in our rooms and wait for a lightning bolt. Sometimes, we have to make a courageous, bold move to kick start someone *else's* boldness, too.

Start a blog? *Why the hell not?* Sure, it's friggin' HARD, especially in today's day and age. Everyone and their mom has a blog, and there is just SO much that you've gotta know to get the ball rolling.

But there's this thing called Google, and it's pretty helpful. You get started the same way as anyone else—by having an idea, and deciding to make it happen. Then, you research. You do your due diligence like anyone else, too, to learn the ropes—we all start somewhere! Don't "have time?" No one does. You don't have time, you make time. It's what you choose to do within each 24-hour time frame that determines the layout of your life. Quite frankly, no one is liked by everyone. It's not about the follower count—heck, Jesus started with only 12.

Fear stops us from doing what we are destined to do.

Similarly, perfectionism stops us from doing what we have to do. Really, perfectionism is just a fear of being imperfect, of being and/or showing flaws. It's silly, since we are ALL flawed! Except Chris Hemsworth. Not flawed.

There's getting it perfect, and there's getting it done. One is nearly impossible to attain, especially on the reg, and keeps us stagnant and stressed out. The other is essential to any progress in our lives, because it's a matter of *doing* rather than *waiting*.

You've just gotta start, and you've gotta start now. Why the hell not?

UNBALANCE THE SCALE

In one of my weekly internet perusings, I found myself reading a blog post for "recovering perfectionists" (Hello, this is me) and the author hit the nail so far on the head it split straight through the wood of my soul (dramatic, but true):

"Balance is a code name for that dirty word, perfection."

Oof. Perfection. My skin is already crawling. But DING DING DING, she was right on the money.

Every article and its mother online paints this completely impractical, nearly fantastical picture of "balance." We think of balance as this achievable feat that starts with a 6 a.m. wake up for devotional and coffee before the kids are off to school, followed by a productive day of building your budding empire of a business (which just hit a new revenue goal—go you!), coming home to whip up something Pioneer Woman-worthy right in time for your honey's arrival home. Your kindergartener is in bed by 8 p.m., and you're unplugged from technology and focused on "us time" by 8:30 for a romantic movie-in-bed kinda wind-down. Heck, you might even squeeze in a facemask, because pores are important and #selfcare.

L-O-FRIGGIN-L. Amiright???

I can't even tell you how many times I've written out the perfect to-do list for the day, packed with #AllTheThings, for it to come crashing and burning down by 10 a.m. Then, instead of being a Balanced Brittany, I'm a Panicking Priscilla, freaking the freak out that everything is already "off-schedule" and falling to bits and I didn't even make it to a mid-morning snack.

The problem: the "perfect" to-do list doesn't exist.

Nor does the perfect day. Or the perfect balance. Or the perfect anything.

Balance, by nature, is perfect; it's a perfect tightrope walk, lest the scale fall. We wonder why we feel such pressure and anxiety all the friggin' time whenever we're trying to maintain this perfected act? Because it's not only hard—it's impossible. Balance is a unicorn. Embrace the balancing ACT, knowing and understanding that it's all just that: an act. Instead of saying we're clinging to some semblance of "balance" in our lives, let's cut the crap entirely and call it what it is: UNBALANCE.

It's time to unbalance the scale.

Balance implies that all things are somehow receiving equal weight. But that, by nature—in this thing called REAL LIFE—is impossible.

Unless someone's got cloning down pat, we cannot physically be doing multiple things at the same time. We can't even be THINKING about multiple things at the same time, or we're scientifically proven to be less productive. So DOING multiple things at once? I mean, nada.

We need to unbalance the scale.

Let some things be more important in some moments than others.

It's unpractical and illogical to think that we can make it happen for all things all the time. At any given moment, we're "balancing" all of the different buckets in our life: job, relationship, faith, chores, kids, friends, self. For a mom to be fully focused on her kids, she cannot also be fully focused on reconciling the family finances. For a business owner to be fully focused on prepping the next launch, she cannot also be writing the daily company blog or catching up on the phone with her girlfriend. If one thing takes, another gives. It's the balancing act—or unbalance—of life.

Sometimes, life happens. SH*T happens. On any given day, your perfectly balanced scale could be balancing away and an imaginary, screaming toddler (or heck, a very real screaming toddler) could come barreling through the room, smacking that scale to kingdom come. Attention is needed elsewhere, balance is lost, and all you're left with is a cup of coffee that's a) cold and b) all over your shirt.

People get sick. Accidents happen. Spouses fight. Businesses struggle. When the unexpected hits, so too does the reality that balance is but a mystical, glittery unicorn that passes by in our dreams. Trying to plan a balanced life is like trying to plan the perfect life, free from curveballs. Which just…ain't how this game of life works. The problem isn't (I think) just in the fact that we're biologically incapable of multitasking efficiently. I mean, don't get me wrong, if someone could swear by multitasking, it would be me. I'd be fooling myself, though, since science swears I can't do it (and neither can you). The problem is in this societal pressure to "be balanced."

Aka, "be perfect." Have it all together. Because if/when you do, the gears will magically click and VOILA: peace and harmony will exist, if only for a moment. Then the moment is gone, and you have to do it all over again. Y'all, balance is exhausting.

Imbalance, though—imbalance breeds discipline.

By being off-balance and by acknowledging our imbalance, we're forced to ACTUALLY PRIORITIZE our lives. We're forced to say, you know what? This takes precedence right now, and that takes precedence next, and it is all A-OK.

Imbalance breeds contentment.

Which is kind of ironic, since we're led to THINK that this whole "balance" lie is what brings about joy. NOSIREE—don't believe it. In fact, "balance" brings about dissatisfaction, since it is—once again—impossible to truly grasp, and impossible to maintain. imbalance—and more so, the acceptance of our unbalanced lives as beautiful—allows us to come closer to feelings of contentment in our everyday life instead of constantly thinking/worrying/wondering about how we can/should/might be adding or subtracting to get to some acceptable level of balanced Zen.

Unbalance breeds freedom.

Say buh-bye to those feelings of being attached by a lead thread to your planner, lest one thing fall off course and the scales break. Instead, welcome an unbalanced scale with open arms. Because hey, that's real life, yo! With that comes the freedom

to unabashedly and unashamedly give some
things more time than others, just because
in that moment, that's what's needed most.

"It's impractical and illogical to think that we can make it happen for all things all the time."

#CAFFEINATEYOURSOUL

Happy Monday! Let's break it down for story time before diving into this week's Monday Mantra.

Back in the day, there was to be a battle between the Philistines and the Israelites. The Philistines chose a champion fighter to represent them, measuring what would be nine feet, three inches by today's standards (holy tall), covered in armor and impressive weaponry.

Enter, Goliath.

Goliath was intimidating AF, to say the least. He told King Saul to send someone out to fight him. I mean…thanks but no thanks, amiright?? If someone could kill him, they would all become his servants. But if HE won, Israel would be THEIR servants.

Enter, David.

David was a young shepherd boy. Basically, the total physical opposite of a literal armored giant. When David came to Saul, Saul started explaining the 52 and then some reasons why he thought David could NOT slay Goliath. Namely that Goliath was—oh I dunno—a champion warrior and David was…not.

But David wasn't having it.

He was convinced that a few things were on his side. 1) His experience as a shepherd. If/when lions or tigers or bears (oh my!) came to mess with his father's flock, he would be the one to chase and strike them down to save the lamb. 2) His faith in God. "The Lord, who saved me from the paw of the lion and from the paw of the bear, will save me from the hand of this Philistine." He believed he COULD, and we all know how that Pinterest quote ends…

Enter today's Monday Mantra: Slay your Goliath.

I think we all know how the story goes at this point, yeah? David with his five stones and slingshot approached Goliath head-on (literally), slingshotting a single stone straight into his forehead…killing him.

He knew that taking the expected route wouldn't work with Goliath. Nor would coming to Goliath's playing field, since the dude had a bit of an obvious advantage right outta the gate (hello, he could smoosh the kid instantly). David couldn't compare to Goliath in terms of strength or shield or power or might. He COULD, however, think outside the box and bring something new to the field that was special to his own skill set that would be the real difference-maker.

I don't even think this dude knew what a slingshot WAS, let alone expected it to be his kryptonite. So, Goliath fell. David slayed Goliath, and we have every right and ability to slay our own Goliaths—to pull a David on 'em—in our own way. Whether our Goliath is a literal person, a horrible job, a hard choice, a medical diagnosis, or some other challenging test entirely, we know 'em, we have 'em, we fight 'em.

To slay your Goliath rests on a few key things:

- **Adaptability**

- **Choice**

Adaptability beats strength when strength does not adapt. Your Goliath could feel far beyond the physical specs of David's Goliath. Your Goliath could feel taller, broader, stronger, mightier, whatever. But like David, your Goliath might lack adaptability. If you can think outside the box to beat your own Goliath, you just might find your secret sauce for success by the end of the fight. Of course, adaptability does not mean changing the Goliath. As I'm sure you know well, some Goliaths ARE Goliaths to us because of how stinkin' stubborn and unchangeable they are or feel. So it's not up to THEM to adapt.

It's up to US. It's up to us to figure out how we even can adapt in the situation to not only beat Goliath in the end, but to be and stay okay through the fight. That might mean adapting physically, but it might mean adapting mentally or emotionally to change the way we were thinking about Goliath in the first place, to reframe the fight to something winnable for us. Mentally shrinking Goliath might not LITERALLY lessen his size, but it very well might make us a helluvah lot more likely to approach the giant head-on in the first place.

Then there's the whole "choice" factor. The most successful folks in life are often the grittiest. They're the ones who choose to be successful, and settle for no lesser choice. They choose to work, they choose to fight, they choose to trust God along the way. They also choose to embrace the unknown next steps, knowing that sometimes the challenge ahead is an essential mountain to summit before the picture-perfect view. Like the quote often thrown on tanks for the gym: If it does not challenge you, it cannot change you.

We have to choose to not only allow ourselves to be challenged, but to allow ourselves to be changed in the process. Change isn't easy OR comfy, but it is necessary for us to live the best damn lives we could possibly be living. Change takes choice. Oftentimes, that choice is an action. It's a strong, definitive action, as bold-feeling as showing up to battle against an armed giant with nothing but a rubber band and some rocks.

Confronting our fears. Defeating our demons. Rising from our failures. Growing through our pains. Silencing our critics (including the critics in our own heads). Beating the odds. Blossoming amidst the dirt and thorns.

Since David versus Goliath IS one of the most popular Bible stories ever, it's only fitting to drop a verse for ya: "The Lord your God who goes before you will himself fight for you." (Deuteronomy 1:30)

Think about it. Pray about it…isn't it something special?

No matter how giant your Goliath, you are not alone. You are never alone. Your fight is not yours alone.

God will always help us slay our giant, but we still have to show up to the fight, stones in hand. David had full faith in God, but he brought five smooth stones with him to the battlefront; he didn't show up empty-handed, expecting a lightning bolt from heaven to take care of Goliath on his behalf. God will fight for us, but we're in it together. Against any Goliath, we aren't called to sit back and let God swoop in on a white horse to take over while we meekly watch from a safe, comfy distance.

Nope. We're called to take God with us into battle. We're called to trust that God will 1) be there in the first place, and 2) guide our path and decisions and thoughts to eventual victory. We're called to never believe that God is abandoning us in our scariest, hardest moments, but to always hold onto hope that He is right there next to us, equipping our minds and hearts for the next move.

Is your slingshot ready? It's time to slay your Goliath.

CHECK-IN!

1. List 5 things you're grateful for:

2. What have you made happen so far this year?

3. What WILL you make happen?

4. Which Mantra has spoken the loudest to you so far?

5. What NOISE in your life can you intentionally turn down?

Rest
REFOCUS
Restart

REST, REFOCUS, RESTART

Sometimes, the thing we must do most is reset, refocus, restart. (In that order, rinse and repeat).

Have you ever experienced. . .the screen of death?

If you have, at this point you're probably already groaning or shuddering recalling the horrors. I have been so unfortunate as to have had not one, not two, but THREE run-ins with said screen in the past year alone. The last time it happened was during a blur of a hot mess express week. I was having a near-meltdown at our kitchen table, surrounded by too many papers with too many to-dos. As Friday went on and I was attempting to get wrapped up for the weekend, the unthinkable happened…the blinking computer screen of death.

The past few times this screen happened, it turned out to be a manufacturer malfunction on that specific piece of hardware (super), so it called for a constant back-and-forth to Best Buy and consistently sending it out to Kentucky for service before they came to the conclusion that I just needed to purchase a brand new computer (super duper). Fast forward to being on a brand spankin' new laptop, you can maybe imagine the wicked fast rush of not-so-good emotions (and swear words, sorry Mom) that came to me the second my screen started freaking the freak out again.

…No bueno, mi amigos. Fast forward again, and I was thiiiiiiis close to what I thought was malfunction número tres. I had been bopping about all weekend long, and was understandably spent by the time Sunday night was rolling around. I was feverishly trying to upload video content on my phone, when suddenly, the sound on my phone just stopped working. No sign ahead of time, no hardware issue, no other problems ever—it just decided it didn't want to play or record sound. I was about to just call it quits and literally "try again tomorrow," when I realized it was like Part Two of the Week's Lesson:

"Reset, refocus, restart."

When my laptop went bezerk, my gut instinct was to panic, but some semblance of grace deep down served as a friendly and necessary reminder: Shut it down. Hit restart.

So simple, but so often forgotten…and so needed.

I hadn't actually shut down my laptop in God only knows how long, so it's no surprise that it decided to end the week on a spastic note. Similarly, with my phone, I never actually turn it off—it just alternates between being on and in use, and on and charging up. None of my devices ever get a friggin' BREAK. They just go-go-go as fast and as much as I make them. Poor things.

Once I closed out the 52 and then some tabs I had open and actually shut down… wouldn't ya know, the screen calmed down. At first I was nervous; I initially tried re-opening everything immediately upon restart, and there was a flicker or two that kept me on edge. So I figured I should give it a rest (good thought, E) and stop opening every tab. I should treat my tech the way we should treat ourselves—with grace and with due rest. Wouldn't you know, it hasn't flickered or blinked or flashed scary lines of colorful death since. (Bless up.)

Similarly with my phone, I was on Multitasking Madwoman mode. I was trying to upload Stories to Instagram, watch Stories ON Instagram, record video, like pictures, check my email, and answer texts all at the same dang time. Like, who in their right mind…?!?

So I stopped.

I exited out of everything. I gave it a hot sec to regroup. When I came back to it, lo and behold, THE SOUND WORKED. Just like technology wasn't programmed to be "on" forever, neither were we.

For as much as we think we can power through, we can't power through without ever powering off.

Instead of aligning our sails towards hustle island, we need to RE-align to an island of actual peace and quiet, to effectively regroup and get back to best self.

Reset, refocus, restart.

As much as we may want to be Superwoman—and for as much as we may think we ARE Superwoman sometimes—we can't be Superwoman all the time. Just like Superman needs to be Clark Kent, we too need to de-cape and chill the heck out once in a while so that we can be even MORE super the next time around.

We've gotta let ourselves reset.

Then realign with our purpose (our WHYs).

Also refocus on our goals.

Before hitting restart and getting back to business as usual.

Reset. Realign. Refocus. Restart.

Great things take time. Give yourself that time this week to reset, realign, refocus, restart strong.

GREAT
things
TAKE TIME

3
4
5
6
7
8
9

Great things take time. How many times have ya heard it in life so far?? Chances are, quite a bit. It's a commonly thrown around phrase that lacks the punch it once packed. It was basically turned into a societal cliché to get us overly ambitious folks to turn it TF down when we're on a real roll. If you're ambitious and you know it, say HOLLAH. (Hollah!)

I get it—I feel you.

But that doesn't make it any less easy to really believe, especially when we want it all and we want it now. When we're developing discipline and doing everything in our reasonable power to affect the outcome of a situation, we expect results. Oftentimes, we expect to see 'em when we wanna see 'em, or when we think we SHOULD be seeing 'em, and not whenever the heck they decide to come about "in due time." So great things take time can be a harder one to stomach for those of us on the train of fast 'n' furious growth, committed to

blossom until the day we die (guilty). We get that great things take time for most, but we think we somehow possess this superhuman trait that allows us an extra somethin' somethin'. Or rather, we think we should be going faster/further/fiercer just because we are who we are, and then we get down on ourselves if/when we take a bit more time than we had allotted in our brain to make it happen. When really, great things actually take time and it's A-okay if that "time" in reality doesn't align with the time that we had randomly set in our brains as being reasonable or rational for achieving XYZ.

We only have so much in our immediate control. Sure, we can impact the outcome of one thing or another by our actions today and our decisions tomorrow, but some of the greatest things/successes/achievements in life aren't as predictable or immediately plannable. They require time spent nurturing, fostering, planning, executing to build a series of smaller successes into a bigger great THING.

Good things take hustle. Great things take time.

Good things take hustle, like being good about finishing three loads of laundry on a Saturday afternoon, or getting your errands done, or Marie Kondo'ing your closet.

But great things take time.

Girlfriend, do ya feel the itch?

I've got the itch REAL bad.

The itch to go fast and go far and make it happen…like, yesterday. I swear the dang itch is contagious—there should be some sort of cream for it at this point! Until then, let this be your cream (and friendly daily reminder):

Great things take time.

The greatest of the great were not born overnight. They did not step into success the second they decided they wanted to be successful. Nor did they come into this world already knowing all of the "secrets" to propel them beyond the rest. Sure, some folks might have advantages. Some have connections, relationships, or opportunities that the rest of us just don't have access to, but that's okay. WE might have something that THEY don't have, too. (So never ever begrudge someone their great thing when it comes—just believe yours is coming, too!)

How fast you go does not directly impact how far you make it.

It takes grit and stamina along the way to really make it happen. If we go too fast too soon, we're liable to not end up very far at all before burning out altogether. Don't risk ruining the race by running it too fast straight out of the gate. Let yourself pick up a pace that's right for you, and everywhere you are, have been, and will be throughout the course of it.

It's like a literal marathon—it's not even physically POSSIBLE to run that thing in less than two hours (Google says that the fastest recorded one so far was 2:02:57 by a boss Kenyan). If someone showed up swearing they were going to make it in less—especially without having first trained for

YEARS to make it happen—they'd be nuts. If someone showed up asking how to cut their time in half just because they felt like it, they'd also be nuts. And they'd likely end up injured, defeated, and not at all number one.

If you're going to run a marathon, it takes time.

You train. You start smaller, and you build up to the big day. You can't just show up at the starting line thinking you're going to best the rest because you want to and say so. Sure, you can think good thoughts. You can "manifest" the heck outta it. You can envision yourself winning that dang marathon without having run a single race before in your LIFE. At the end of the day (and race), though, if ya didn't do the necessary prep work, the great thing that could've been won't be nearly as great in reality.

When we rush, we risk missing integral parts of the process. We risk doing more harm than good, skipping steps, and getting sloppy along the way. Great things take time. Don't think your thing is any less great because it took longer than anticipated to get there, and definitely don't think your thing is any less great because it took longer than so-and-so did to get there. Your race is yours and yours alone—nix the comparison (although, that's a mantra for another Monday).

In my time as a blogger, I've gotten tons of emails from fellow or aspiring bloggers, often asking for tips for "quick" success: how to grow by thousands of followers overnight (impossible), how to get paid to post for brands after having just started taking your Instagram seriously (unlikely), ways to leave your job ASAP to blog (unsustainable).

Really, there is no shortcut to true success.

Sure, there are shortcuts to LOOK successful. But those shortcuts are just that—shortcuts. They're not sustainable, and they're sure as heck not true indicators of anything worthwhile. Time is not always a luxury—sometimes, it's a necessity. It's a necessary, unavoidable part of a process that can't be gypped.

So give yourself some credit while you run your race. Good things take hustle, but great things take time.

"Don't think your thing is any less great because it took longer than anticipated to get there, and definitely don't think your thing is any less great because it took longer than so-and-so did to get there."

#CAFFEINATEYOURSOUL

If there's one thing the world needs more of, it's action.

Action, and ice cream sandwiches.

At the end of the day, it can become too easy to feel defeated, overwhelmed, and all sorts of other Negative Nelly feels. Sunday nights used to give me so much anxiety. It used to be crippling, but now it can be motivating. I'm always completely slapped in the face with approximately 32 different ideas, to-dos, and tidbits of inspiration… right before bedtime. If I tried to get everything tackled and conquered right then and there, that might not work out too well. Chances are I won't finish, and I'll just end up exhausted and overwhelmed to start the week…no bueno. But at the same time, sitting there just thinking of all the things without acting on any of them could be just as overwhelming—and even more unproductive.

Also, at the end of the day, the most motivating thing for a Monday isn't the Hallmark-card quote that gives the warm and fuzzy feels for a passing hot sec. If it doesn't inspire you to DO something about it…then I don't really know how motivating it was in the first place. The most motivating thing makes you act on it. Makes you want to make it happen.

You know that really big, totally scary, kinda intimidating but really powerful dream you have in your heart?

…Yeah, that one.

What are you gonna do about it?

The sad truth: Approximately not-nearly-enough percent of people are action takers. There are dreamers and there are doers: the folks who dream and let their dreams stay up in dreamland, and the folks who dream and then DO—the folks who act on dreams to bring them down from dreamland to reality. Girlfriend, if you don't DO something about your dream…what the heck do you think is gonna happen to it?

The hard truth: Your dream will never

come true if you don't MAKE it come true. Too often, we depend on other people to make OUR dreams happen. But that ain't gonna work. Other people have other dreams, wants, desires, needs that aren't our dreams—they're THEIRS. We can't expect and/or depend on any sort of help with OURS. Own your dream, and act on it accordingly.

This extends beyond those dreamy sort of dreams we all have and beelines for everyday life.

Have an itch to hit the gym? Act on it. (Work it girl!)

Missing your grandparents' voices? Act on it. (Call them!)

Feeling frumpy in your closet? Act on it. (Treat yo'self to something new!)

Uninspired in your day job? Act on it. (Challenge yourself to make it better in the interim!)

Wanting a date on Friday night? Act on it. (Ask him out! Just do it!)

Feel the urge to pay for the stranger's coffee behind you? Act on it. (It'll make their day.)

Stop looking for the "perfect moment" to make something happen, and start making moments more perfect. Nothing is perfect—most things are far from perfection. It might not feel conventional, easy, comfortable, or ideal. It might feel downright awkward or weird. But until you act on it—and keep acting on it—nothing will change. Nothing will (ever) feel easier, either, unless you act on it over and over again.

When something downright awful happens in the world, everyone jumps to "thoughts and prayers." Don't get me wrong, "thoughts and prayers" are good. But, I mean, they're about as effective as "thinking and praying" about how much you'd like a raise, or how badly you want a date with the cute guy at the coffee shop. I 100 percent believe in the power of prayer, but I believe in prayer coupled with ACTION. God did not make us to sit in a secluded corner of solitude, just praying.

He made us to be prayer warriors, praying for our needs and the needs of others, and then listening to Him and His guidance to get the inspiration we need to ACT ON IT. Warriors don't just sit around "hoping" the enemy is defeated. They take a personal hand in making it happen. Lightning bolts from heaven aren't going to come down to make sh*t happen. WE are going to make sh*t happen, with His help.

Stop searching for "the right time." The right time is today. The right time is now. There will be no better time. No lightning bolt from above that tells you IT IS TIME! Whatever "IT" is on your heart…now's the time to act on it.

BABY, YOU'RE a FIREWORK

BABY, YOU'RE A FIREWORK

(4th of July time)

"Baby, you're a firework…Just own the night // Like the Fourth of July"

Raise your hand if you're now belting Katy Perry in your head. #YoureWelcome. It's a party in the USA! Here comes a lil' patriotic Monday Mantra—break out the sparklers, barbecue, and red, white, and blue! Fun fact: Before the Declaration of Independence was even signed, John Adams envisioned fireworks as being part of the party. Fireworks just scream WOO! They're pretty darn close to magic, if you ask me, and rightly so. We lovelovelove 'em so much because they release what's called "eustress:" a mix of euphoria and positive/pleasant stress that comes when our body experiences fear with the knowledge that we're still safe, like riding a roller coaster. So, this Monday Mantra is dedicated to 'Murica. Baby, you're a firework, in the least-cheesy, least-Katy-Perry way possible. Here's why:

A firework is just a stick before it's lit.

Just this stick full of black powder and a compound, packed with powerful potential. It's got "stars" (the compound mixture), a shell (the container holding the stars), black powder (propellant that ignites), a bursting charge (ignites the stars), a mortar (the tube holding the firework), and a fuse (what gets lit and gives it air time before exploding).

That's it. Before it's lit…that's it, and it's such a transformation from being Exhibit A, a dusty stick, to Exhibit B lighting up a night sky.

People are like that.

First: We've got all of these bits and pieces inside of us, unknown to many— even unknown to ourselves sometimes. We're not just empty shells walking around; we're full of stuff, and potential to explode into whatever direction we set forth. It's this compounded effect of anything and everything we've ever experienced in life up to where we're at right now. Somehow, it all combines perfectly to make us who we are—sometimes jagged around the edges, but perfectly imperfect nonetheless.

But we have to light our own fuses and let our light out.

Cheesy, but true. Your light is that undeniable spark of joy deep down, no matter how deep down it might be right now. That is the essence of your being. It's the IT factor of just being you—the thing that makes you different than the other six to seven billion people on the planet.

Stop waiting for permission from someone else to be your best self, right now.

Don't hold it inside, and don't wait for someone else to light the fuse. Too often, we become afraid or nervous or skeptical of our own success, and we wait for that go-ahead from someone to remind us that is, in fact, okay (and GOOD) to be ourselves, to go as hard and fabulous as possible, to openly live as our best selves. We worry about someone not liking us for it, and we worry about others' insecurities getting the best of them and affecting us. Someone may see you killing it and feel worse about themselves—and maybe they won't like you for it. But at the end of the day, is this your life or theirs? You don't have enough hours in the day to worry about how everyone and their mom will perceive you when you're really sparkling in your own spotlight. Ain't nobody got time for that, and really, it's just not the point of any of it.

Fireworks don't exist to just outshine each other—they exist to all be enjoyed by all different kinds of people in all different kinds of circumstances. You have every right to be your own firework and go as high, fast, and far as you possibly can… and so does the next girl. You can both do it—literally alongside each other—without being consumed by the desire to burn the other out first. Wasting time on that will hurt you, too, and YOU won't shine as brightly or go as high/fast/far, either. It takes energy to burn bright. Use your energy wisely and positively.

There are different kinds of fireworks, of course: different colors, different displays, different shapes, and different sounds. Some high, some low, some crackle, some boom—the whole nine yards. So don't think you need to be like the others.

They perfectly complement the saying, "You can be the sweetest peach, but there's still gonna be someone who doesn't like peaches." Someone is going to prefer the loudest, brightest firework, and another will want the smaller, softer display. It doesn't mean either are better than the other—it just means they shine in different ways, meant for different folks to enjoy.

We don't really see or appreciate fireworks when it's light. We need darkness to fully appreciate them.

Sometimes, a person's true colors don't always show in the light. Similarly, sometimes the best of you can come out in the worst of situations—the light is revealed in the dark.

When you see someone else sparkling in the light of an achievement or win, don't begrudge them or internalize it at all as reflective of your own success or lack thereof. Just see it, acknowledge it, compliment it, admire it. Hope that it goes as high as it should. View it as an objective third party outsider with a heart.

Then, keep focusing on your own firework.

Keep working on what's on your own inside, so that your outside is set for the most colorful, glorious, joyful explosion when your own time comes.

Baby, you're a firework. Don't forget it.

Choose the Chase

CHOOSE THE CHASE

Ever get the Sunday Scaries? You know. . . that all-too-familiar anxiety that bombards your brain as soon as Sunday starts leaning towards Monday. Ew. I used to get hit hard with major anxiety every Sunday night. Then, come Monday morning, it would feel like an impossible chase and race to get #AllTheThings accomplished. Finish weekend chores? Catch up on blog work? Inbox zero? Get ahead on any work? Grocery shopping? There comes a point when you realize there are just so many things, and ain't nobody got time.

You've gotta choose.

Chase perfection of it all, or chase happiness through it all.

Enter, today's Monday Mantra: Choose the chase—the chase of perfection, or the chase of happiness.

You cannot choose both chases, because they're two different paths less traveled.

One, though, is impossible. It's a never-ending path, because it can never be realized; there is never an end point or final destination. That path is perfection, and its chase is a setup for failure from the get-go.

No matter how hard you try to become "perfect," it's just not going to happen. It's not going to happen for any of us. The only perfect being out there died on a cross some 2,000 years ago. Perfection is this totally unattainable, staged idea in society that typically only drives us perfectionists nuts when we inevitably fall short at something. While it can be arguably good to chase after perfection in the spirit of self-betterment, I don't know many perfectionists who are admittedly okay with falling short. I've been a perfectionist since the womb, and it drives me nuts if I don't hit my own arbitrarily assigned standards. The chase for perfection goes on and on, but with every shortcoming comes the risk of thinking less of yourself—even considering the f-word (that's failure, folks).

Perfection is not the chase to choose.

The other chase, though, is possible every single moment of every single day.

It's never ending, but it's more satisfying, because you can make it happen in the moments that matter most. Enter: happiness.

You see, happiness and joy are two different things. When they say "choose happiness," it can be hard, since happiness is temporal. Happiness comes and goes; happiness comes, happiness goes, sadness comes, and sadness goes, then happiness is back at it again. To choose happiness every day can really feel like this constant chase, and here's the deal: it is. It's a constant chase in pursuit of something that makes you feel good in some way in the moment. Maybe it's happiness in your job, maybe it's in your relationship...or it's the happiness that comes from finding a 70 percent off sale, stumbling upon Halo Top at your grocery store (bless), or getting new workout clothes that make you feel hot AF.

The chase to choose happiness is a lot more satisfactory than chasing perfection.

Happiness can be found in the seemingly smallest of moments if only we remember to acknowledge it as it comes. I don't think of it as this deep satisfaction—that's where joy comes in. It's the tiny bits of joy and, well, happiness, that come in little moments along the way. Happiness is subject to YOUR guidelines and yours alone. What makes you happy isn't necessarily what makes someone else happy, and that's A-okay. You can't necessarily control what makes you happy—you just feel it.

Perfection, on the other hand, is oftentimes driven entirely by outside influence, whether we realize it or not. We judge our own perfectionism based on how it "measures up" to society's status quo—what we deem to be "better" or "best"—and we compare that to where we're at now. Then, we judge ourselves. We consider ourselves to be less-than-perfect, and we risk that trickling down into less-than-worthy. The cycle of negativity starts there, and we're left feeling perpetually dissatisfied with ourselves and our lives when we continually fail to reach this impossible pinnacle of perfectionism.

Ain't nobody got time.

Choose the chase.

Choose happiness.

The moment you realize that you can find something happy in every moment, the moment your life becomes a helluvah lot happier.

Granted, of course not everything in life is happy.

Sometimes, life sucks. There are totally awful, sad, heartbreaking, uncontrollable circumstances that come before us that we've gotta face, and it's not always easy, fun, or anything close to happy.

So…the chase continues.

Every rose has its thorn. For every downside, there's an upside. Even if that upside is as seemingly simple and small as "I woke up today and have another day to try again." Some people don't even get that.

So, keep choosing the chase. Choose happiness. Keep choosing to chase that which can be attained time and time again, and acknowledge it in your life. Collect happy moments and hold onto them for all they're worth, then go out and spread them around for others to pick up, too.

You choose the chase.

I WILL politely PERSIST

I WILL POLITELY PERSIST

Another Monday, another day of feeling dread that the weekend is over, drowned by the fullness of your plate (already), and general worry about the week ahead, where anything besides a persistently refilled coffee mug feels like the biggest chore amiright?

I think we've all taken a ride on the Monday morning struggle bus before, and we can say that it's definitely not the ride of choice (Can there be a Monday Porsche? Asking for a friend).

But whether it's Monday morning, Hump Day night in a looooong week, or Saturday afternoon post-brunch, there's one thing we all could really use a bit more of when the going gets tough: persistence.

Sometimes, we feel the pressures of society and the world all around us, telling us that we're not good enough, not strong enough, not smart enough to actually achieve what we really want to achieve. We're told that unless we're hustling 24/7, we'll be out-hustled and inevitably fall

short. We know how badly we want our own dreams, but we're told others want it more. We feel like unless we in turn rise to the occasion and match everyone else and their mom's level of hustle, we won't be able to get where we want to go in work, life, and even in love.

So, we're hit with a big fat, "Is it worth it?" Is the sacrifice worth it? IS there sacrifice involved? How do I handle the uncertainties and fears? What happens when I feel like I've reached the end of my rope?

Enter, today's Monday Mantra: "I will politely persist."

Internalize this like it's yo' JOB this week, wouldja???

I will keep going, and when I feel like stopping, I'll just go even farther.

I will persist, even when I feel like pressing pause. When my dreams feel too high in the sky, I'll be persistent knowing that if I shoot for the moon and miss, I'll still be in the sky among the stars.

I say "politely," because there's a right and a wrong way to persist. Persisting like a bulldog won't necessarily get you very far in the long run. Sure, it might push a few roadblocks out of the way now, but it might plow over the wrong peeps and strike the match to bridges that shouldn't be burned.

Being an asshat won't get you very far. When in doubt, always be polite.

Dedicate yourself to politely persisting towards every goal, dream, intention, and desire that you've outlined. Because you are capable, you are worthy, and you should be done playing small (like, right this very second). Instant success isn't the only kind of success.

You know the stories, I'm sure:

If Henry Ford hadn't persisted, there would be no Ford Motor Company.

If Oprah hadn't persisted after being fired from her first TV anchor job, there would be no Oprah. Literally.

If J.K. Rowling hadn't persisted after countless editor rejections, there would be no Harry Potter.

If Walt Disney hadn't persisted after being told he lacked imagination, there would be no Mickey Mouse.

If Thomas Edison hadn't persisted after God only knows how many actual attempts at the lightbulb, there would be no ELECTRICITY.

Stories of seemingly abysmal failure turned into the greatest success stories we know today.

Rejection. Heartbreak. Loss. Humiliation. All taken and transformed into a lesson to be learned and some of the most epic stories of all time, because someone decided to politely persist at their passion until something happened.

Here's the key: You have to want it so badly that being persistent doesn't faze you.

You have to want it so badly that being persistent isn't intimidating or annoying—it's warmly welcomed as a necessary stepping stone on the way to making it happen. Want it badly enough that you're dying to take another step—the next step—to follow up, make some tweaks, talk to more people about the dream and why it's worthwhile.

Your dream isn't any less valuable, meaningful, or worthwhile than Henry Ford's dream, Oprah's dream, or Walt Disney's dream.

If they had quit, we wouldn't have even KNOWN their dreams, because the billion-dollar empires that resulted might not have come to fruition. We wouldn't be sitting here chatting about their successes, because they would've stopped at one or two failures. If you want to be talked about later, you've gotta be willing to fail and persist now.

The people who win aren't the people who've never lost. They're just the people who have lost and persisted anyway.

You and your dreams are worth it as much as J.K. Rowling's dream for the world to know the Boy Who Lived. They're as worthy as a talking mouse with big ears, too. They're worth your time, effort, intention, and hard work.

They're worth politely persisting.

So keep on going, and keep persisting until you Make. It. Happen.

I REFUSE

→ to play ←

SMALL

I REFUSE TO PLAY SMALL

On the corkboard smack-dab in front of my face at my desk, I have a hot pink Post-It note that says, "STOP PLAYING SMALL. You've got this." At first, I wasn't 100 percent sure how much I'd need a mantra like that. I figured it felt a bit cliché; in the moments when you need it most, hearing, "You got this!" from someone isn't always the most genuinely encouraging or motivating phrase. You're like, "Yeah yeah…I got this and all, but HOW THE HECK AM I GOING TO ACTUALLY DO IT, KAREN?!?"

In the moment, it's easy to shrink.

We shrink—we cower back from our own potential.

Sometimes, it's in fear of failing.

Other times, it's in fear of actually succeeding. The truth is that as much as it might suck to be living stagnant in our sameness, it's scary to think we might actually make our dreams come true and live with the responsibility of making them

work or seeing them fall apart before our very eyes.

But here's the kicker: It's impossible to grow and evolve and truly make it happen in the mindset that you're too small and unworthy for your dreams.

It's time to refuse to play small.

It's easy to dream. It's easy to sit back and think, "Wouldn't it be nice to do _____ ? Wouldn't it be nice to live like _____ ? If only I had _____, then I'd be doing/making/rocking it!" But oftentimes, we actually have way more options in our toolkit to take a step—any step—in a direction pointed towards making those dreams and goals happen. We COULD settle for more. We COULD start small and get big quicker rather than later.

Why, then, instead of actively pursuing our dreams and goals, do we let ourselves become distracted by worries and what-ifs and insecurities, or take steps that don't actually matter at all? We don't do the "hard" things that are required to get from point A to point B (even though we can do hard things). Because at the end of the day, sometimes it's easier to complain about how we wish things were different than it is to buckle up and just get it done.

Here's the thing: It feels easier in the moment to just wish for greatness, but it's harder to swallow the failure pill than it is to just do the damn work from the start.

We play small, because it feels easier in the moment then playing big.

But you're worth more than that. You've gotta refuse to play small. You've gotta dream so big that you have no choice but to start working on it ASAP, and you've gotta want it so bad that the work doesn't scare you.

Playing small feels comfortable. Playing small feels easier and more attainable, because it allows us to just go by in a very comfy cozy way, not really changing anything about our current lifestyle in pursuit of this new status or accomplishment. But nothing good ever happens in comfort zones; you can't expect to live a new-and-improved job/income/status/LIFE if you aren't willing to step outside of your current box, make some positive changes, experience growing pains, and up-level to new heights.

You need to refuse to play small in order to open yourself up to being big.

Stop letting yourself cower in the corner of fear to pursue your real dreams. There could always be fear in life, but there could also always be hope. Choose hope, choose positivity, and choose to go after both intentionally.

Stop masking your inaction as busy-ness or broke-ness. If you want it badly enough, make the time and/or make the money to make it happen. When there's a will, there's a way, and if there's no way just yet, at least there's Google.

Stop playing small. You deserve more than that. You owe your greatness not only to yourself, but to all of the people you could be blessing in life by sharing it around.

Stop playing small. You've got this.

"You've gotta dream so big that you have no choice but to start working on it ASAP, and you've gotta want it so bad that the work doesn't scare you."

#CAFFEINATEYOURSOUL

I WAS BORN TO STAND OUT

I WAS BORN TO STAND OUT

"Why are you trying so hard to fit in when you were born to stand out?"

If you know exactly what movie that quote is from, we just became best friends.

Let me ask you a question.

How many times do you feel yourself giving in to what-ifs, fear, and anxiety of the unknown?

Too often (like, waaaaaay too often), we're faced with so much self-doubt. We've got these dreams—these really friggin' BIG dreams!—and we don't know if we can bring them to fruition.

We don't know if we can do it.

It's a big fat BUT WHAT IF I FAIL that looms over our heads, making it hard to move forward with certainty—sometimes, move forward at all.

We're afraid of standing out.

We're afraid of putting our deepest desires and dreams and wants out there in the open, because then THEY stand out. We know that when we stand out, we're up for criticism. We face the naysayers, doubters, and straight-up mean people who would rather see us fail than lift us up.

I mean, we ALL have that person. Heck, for some of us, it might be a family member. That uncle at family dinners who thinks you're nutty for quitting corporate America to sell makeup? Yeah, no bueno.

So we cower down.

We stifle our own lights, because sometimes it feels easier to burn low and slow on the backburner rather than bright and hot and fast for all to see. It feels easier to chalk it up to wanting to be humble, or not wanting to burn out altogether. That's cheating yourself, because here's the thing:

We were born to stand out. YOU were born to stand out, like we learned alongside Amanda Bynes in 2003's smash chick flick *What A Girl Wants*.

Stop thinking that your life will be easier or better by intentionally avoiding the spotlight.

If anything, you're doing the world a disservice. When you have something really good, meaningful, and worthwhile to offer (Which you do! I know you do!), holding back doesn't help anyone. It doesn't help you, and it sure as heck doesn't help the people who could be really benefiting from the goodness you bring to the table. By being unafraid to stand out, to make mistakes, to learn and grow and blossom with others taking notice, you're giving yourself permission to live your best life.

And you know what? By giving yourself permission to live your best life, you're giving others permission to live their best lives, too.

It's time you refuse to play small, and vow to settle for more. Subjecting yourself to standing out may sometimes feel like you're subjecting yourself to scrutiny, judgment, and unwanted opinions. But honestly…those will always be there, everywhere, all the time.

Because there are asshats in the world.

But for every asshat, I like to think that there are at least two NON-asshats—people who celebrate your goodness instead of squash it, and people who WANT you to stand out instead of cower behind them. People who don't feel so insecure that they just hope for your failure, but people who want you to succeed with every ounce of their being, just as much as they want their OWN success. People who understand that their own success is not dependent on your failure. Those are, in fact, mutually exclusive.

So, stand out.

Stand out with confidence, knowing that you can stand out AND she can stand out, and you can stand out for different reasons or even the same reason. Remember, community trumps competition. You're both individuals on this planet of so many, and you both can and SHOULD stand out somehow, for your own individual goodness. Standing out doesn't mean being cocky, arrogant, narcissistic, or self-centered. Standing out means unabashedly being yourself, celebrating the uniqueness of YOU, and sharing that uniqueness for the betterment and encouragement of everyone around you.

It's really that simple.

You, just as you are, are amazing. So totally amazing, and so totally worthy, too. You were born to stand out. You were born to live life as the individual that you are— as the flamingo in a flock of pigeons, as the fruit loop in the bowl of Cheerios, as every other cliché metaphor says so rightfully so. You were born to stand out, because there is only one of you on this entire planet—one of you in a sea of seven billion. Girlfriend, I think that's pretty darn incredible. If you can't take it from me, take it from one of the biggest, smartest, wisest legends of all time, Dr. Seuss: "Why fit in when you were born to stand out?"

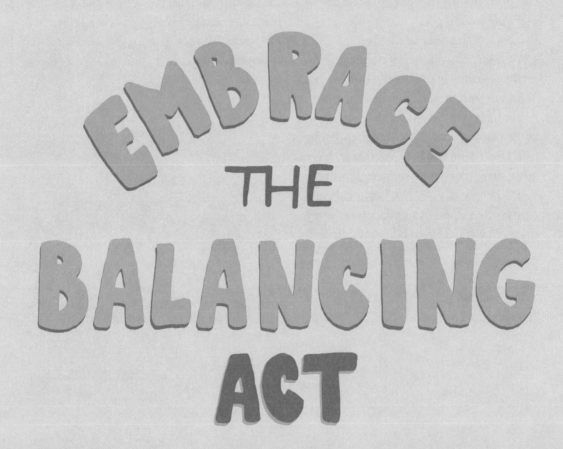

EMBRACE THE BALANCING ACT

If there's one thing I can say with 100 percent certainty that I typically don't have, it's balance. Or, at least, a true sense of it. When you're a naturally ambitious person with a case of way-too-many things on your plate at any given moment, it's the biggest b-word in the book: balance. Google defines it as: an even distribution of weight enabling someone or something to remain upright and steady.

I define it as a unicorn.

Balance is a unicorn.

It's all nice and cute to talk about and we all want it, and it's the cool thing to have or think you have. But in reality…balance just doesn't freakin' exist.

A balancing ACT, on the other hand, that's so very real.

It's so very real—as real as musical theater—because it's all an act. Going through the actions and motions in an attempt to hit this momentary place of equilibrium is a real journey (and real struggle) that we face every single day as we can attempt to "balance" everything from family to friends, work to play, vegetables to ice cream, water to wine. In the end, it's all an act. I don't know, in fact, if I've ever met a single person in the history of ever who could honestly say that he or she had it all figured out, and that their life was totally balanced out, fairly, evenly, and equally. Where weight was equally distributed across all important things, or where different elements are in the "correct" proportions, as Google instructs.

Balance is a unicorn, and balance is an act.

We've gotta embrace the balancing act of life if we ever hope to achieve some semblance of sanity, and if we ever hope to be legitimately stress and anxiety-free, without a constant worry that we're giving too much or too little to one thing or another.

Embrace the balancing act.

Sometimes, certain things basically

demand more attention and time, so balance may not necessarily be about the amount of time spent. It's also about balancing your spirit and achieving that spiritual balance that brings you peace and clarity. It's about balancing your mind and heart, to feel relaxed and stop the 24/7 spinning of to-dos in your brain. The idea of balance may change weekly, daily—even hourly!—and we just have to be flexible enough to go with the flow of it.

One week you might work much more than you play.

One day might be spent entirely relaxing with friends.

One hour might be cheese curls and *Gossip Girl*, while the next is a protein smoothie and yoga.

Maybe you'll nix yoga altogether and opt for a night on the couch with your main squeezes Ben & Jerry…and you know what???

It's totally okay.

As F. Scott Fitzgerald hit square on the head, "Too much of anything is bad, but too much champagne is just right." Some things in life make for a good occasional overindulgence. The key is recognizing which of those things are worth it for you, and not looking back with the slightest bit of regret when you treat yo'self to some quality R&R over extra hours at the office. Embrace the balancing act. Know that balance is not this place beyond golden gates that you reach and get to hang out in forever once you're there.

…Google is smart. Balance: to keep or put something in a steady position so that it does not fall.

Enter, the balancing act. Even Google knows we don't all have our ish totally together, where the pieces of the pie charts of our lives are proportioned our perfectly. Really, at the end of the day, sometimes it's about juggling it all in a way so that it does not fall—so that we don't lose pieces of our puzzles along the way. Because balance is fleeting. Balance is a unicorn, but it's also a butterfly. A gentle, fleeting butterfly. If you hold on too tight, it's suffocated and lost—it only exists to be enjoyed temporarily while it's there.

Chances are, you're never gonna feel like you totally have your shit together. Excuse my French, but it's too true to tone down.

Balance is an act, and balance needs to be acted out time and time again to get it and keep it and enjoy it repeatedly. Google says that balance means everything has to be in "correct proportions," but I think the caveat there is "correct proportions for you at that given moment given all the other things going on in life." Give yourself grace. Know that a seeming lack of balance right now in this moment doesn't mean your whole LIFE isn't balanced. Even if your whole life IS outta whack and unbalanced…it doesn't mean you can't get balanced ASAP with a few painless tweaks. (Tweaks might not always be painless, but sometimes a little pain or discomfort just naturally accompanies very necessary growth.) I've said it before and I'll say it again and I'll keep saying it until I'm blue in the face and a billionaire: Balance is a unicorn.

The hard truth: Balance is not always possible, point blank period. Sometimes it's physically, mentally, emotionally impossible (maybe all three?) to have all of your ducks in a row, swimming straight and forward and fast all at the same time. It just ain't gonna happen. So while you have it, embrace it. Enjoy it. When you don't have it…embrace the balancing act along the way.

Clear Out The Clutter

CLEAR OUT THE CLUTTER

What's worse than feeling anxious?

Feeling suffocated.

There's a suffocating sense of drowning that undoubtedly accompanies any clutter in my life. Whether it's clutter on our bedroom floor, in my makeup drawer, on my desk, or in my mind, the clearest shortcut to stress lies in cluttered space. For me, another biggie is tabs…Yup, tabs. As in, browser tabs on the internet. Granted, I've gotten a whole heckuvah lot better recently than I had been in past lives, but ask anyone who knows me well—it's not unusual to have at minimum 100-plus tabs open at one time (in separate windows, of course). YUP. Ridiculous. It got to the point where my computer would crash because it just literally couldn't take the memory space anymore.

My clutter got destructive.

At first, I'd have a quasi-panic attack as all of the open things I thought I desperately needed were lost into cyberspace.

Then, I realized it actually felt REALLY FREAKING GOOD to start fresh, clean, and new. The same kind of cold shock happens when you throw out all of those clothes you haven't touched since high school (Remind me again why they're still in your closet?), or you clean out the fridge of its expired cheese and pickles from 2012. Same goes when you sever ties with toxic "friends" or let go of past habits. At first, it might feel hard—even anxiety-inducing— to let go and part with the mess. But after… it feels oh so good.

It's time to clear out the clutter.

We're not just talkin' physical mess here either, girlfriend. While that's definitely important to address, the real culprit here is all in your head.

When you have too much going on in your physical world around you, it can manifest itself in your head as a big mumbled jumbled up version of life. By the same token, too much up there can come out in the world around you, leaving you with double the mess. Not controlling the amount of stuff in your brain—not prioritizing or organizing it, and not sifting through the important versus very much unimportant things—just leaves you with too much.

That "stuff" becomes mental clutter.

It becomes hard to creatively brainstorm, dream big, imagine possibilities—heck, it becomes hard to just think straight—when we're sucked into a cluttered mental vortex. We're consumed by mental to-dos, driven by anxieties, propelled by fears of failure or forgetting important things…all instead of being the CEO of our own lives. Ridiculous, amiright?

It becomes a swirling hodgepodge of nutso in our heads and on our hearts that just leads to stress and anxiety and worry and exhaustion and all of those no good, very bad symptoms on the fast track to burnout. It has to stop, because ain't nobody got time for burnout.

Don't trick yourself into thinking you're just "busy" when the clutter really points to being unproductive or overworked.

Don't trick yourself into thinking you HAVE to live a certain way to achieve a certain lifestyle or status. LOOKING busy doesn't mean you are actually busy, the same way that looking like a million bucks doesn't mean you HAVE a million bucks. Having a cluttered mind doesn't mean you are failing, nor does having a cluttered space mean you are inherently messy. But it's important to dig deeper, figure out the underlying cause of the clutter, and then CLEAR IT OUT to make way for the bigger and better.

Learn to goal-set strategically. Having 34 goals is okay, but it can make your pretty head swirl. Sit down and prioritize effectively. Be specific, strategic, and smart with goals. "Write a book" isn't nearly as effective as "Edit book chapter 3 and start writing first draft of chapter 4." Mental organization leads to increased productivity. As they say, Rome was not built in a day. Clear out the clutter.

Learn to worry less. Being reasonably nervous about a big task at hand is normal, and a small bit of stress could be a useful fire under the bum for some. Although, more often than not, worrying clutters your mind, heart, and spirit with fears about the future that may not come to pass. Worrying about tomorrow's possible problems robs joy from today. Face what is in front of you at present. Don't clutter your brain with projections and predictions. Worrying causes clutter. Clear out the clutter.

Learn to set aside time to de-clutter. The same way you set aside 10 to 15 minutes per day to pick up loose ends around the house, wash the dishes, or hang up some clothes in your closet, set aside some time for your brain to get back in shape, too. Sit and think, pray, meditate...whatever it is ya gotta do to get everything back in action working smoothly and refreshed. Not taking time for you causes clutter. Clear out the clutter.

Learn to nix gossip, criticism, and comparison. The trifecta! We live in a world driven by the three—the trinity of toxicity that does nothing but clutter our paths. When was the last time that endlessly scrolling social media left you feeling genuinely uplifted and inspired? Lord knows I WISH that were the case, but more often than not, our Instagram-age leaves us feeling insecure in our own ways. No one else's successes or blessings should in any way, shape, or form dampen your own. Our mindless scrolling leads to mindful comparisons that rob us of today's joys if we let them; they cause jealousy, self-criticism, and CLUTTER if we forget our own good things and focus on other people's. Comparisons, criticism, and gossip causes clutter. Clear out the clutter.

When it DOES come to the physical clutter, set clear but realistic goals, then just START already. "Deep clean and organize the entire house this Saturday afternoon" is not a goal—it's a dream. Tackling a massive project like that all at once is likely to just leave you frustrated and exhausted, and you're better off just watching a Hallmark Classic and calling it a night. Start small,

acknowledging and enjoying your progress
one kitchen cabinet at a time before moving
on to the next little victory.

"Don't trick yourself into thinking you're just 'busy' when the clutter really points to being unproductive or overworked."

#CAFFEINATEYOURSOUL

Settle
for
MORE

SETTLE FOR MORE

Ever stop dead in your tracks over some words of wisdom?

I'm not talkin' a "True!" in passing as you Pinterest the night away with inspirational quotes galore.

I'm talkin' a scroll-stopping, almost-spill-your-latte-in-the-middle-of-Target stop, because you're just that moved by some goodness radiating through your iPhone.

I heard a quote recently, and I gasped upon hearing it. It's just so dang good. From our good ol' pal Dr. Phil. He said, "The difference between you and someone you envy is that you settled for less."

Read that humdinger again.

Instead, you've got to settle for more.

You've heard the phrase, "Don't settle for less than you deserve." But honestly, the struggle is real when it comes to actually knowing "what you deserve." I think "what you deserve" is also cyclical and based on so many factors under the sun, so that it

becomes nearly impossible to figure that phrase out with confidence and true clarity.

It's cliché, and ain't nobody got time for cliché. The problem with cliché is that it carries less influence in our brains. At this point, you probably shrug it off whenever someone throws a good ol' "Don't settle for less than you deserve!" your way, and don't really know what it really means in the context of your own life.

Settling for more is stronger.

It says the same thing, but in a more positive, proactive way. Deciding to settle for more requires guts. It means you've gotta work hard, look ahead, look up, look progressively towards your goals and dreams and aspirations, and actually take action to make it all happen. When you've got the right mindset and are living in abundance, you can't focus on what you don't want because you just might actually inspire what you don't want to happen. Instead, it's gotta all be coming up roses up there to really set your life up for the good to come on in.

Think of everything you do like a big self-fulfilling prophecy. Continually focusing on what you don't want (i.e. "Don't settle for less!") doesn't actually help define and drive you towards the "more" you seek.

Then there's the whole "but you don't deserve more"—an internal battle that plagues so many of our minds when we're twisted in knots about how much time/energy/resources to devote to these seemingly far-off dreams and goals on our hearts. Have you fought that battle before? Where you feel that others are surely "more deserving," and you're okay settling for a little less if it means you're being "unselfish," "smart," "practical," or "fill-in-the-blank-with-whatever-other-excuse-you-have-for-not-going-after-your-goals."

Alright alright alriiiiiight, we've gotta have a lil' talk about this one, girlfriend. Because goshdangit, it's time to debunk the myths that live inside your head as to why you don't truly deserve the raise, deserve the dream job, deserve the great love, deserve the amazing house, deserve the fabulous friends…we're done with that. It's so hard to wake up feeling like there's nothing you want more than your dream, whatever that may be—your "more"—and then subsequently thinking that there's probably someone who deserves it more.

Hold up. Deserves what more? A nice place to live? A loving boyfriend? A bonus from your job? A new job altogether? A friend circle who takes you to margaritas on a Tuesday that's not your birthday?… Happiness?????

Girlfriend, no one deserves happiness more than you. No one deserves more more than you. Settling for more is about recognizing your own self-worth and value and going after what you deserve with conviction. Sometimes, the hard truth of the matter is that we don't respect our dreams—our "more"—enough to give them half a waking chance. Sometimes we don't open our eyes enough to see our own goodness. That's so, so, so bad (and unfair), because it sells you short of the more that's out there for you!

You are completely, totally, holistically responsible for your own happiness, and you deserve every ounce of it.

Settling for more is your call to action to create the life you actually want to be living. It's time to raise your expectations of your own life, and your expectations of yourself.

Granted, there's a fine line between opting to settle for more and never truly being happy—never reaching this place of contentment, or never knowing or feeling like you've truly "made it" to this place of more. I can't lie and say I have an answer for that, because I don't, and I don't think anyone really does. There will always be waves when you're feeling super ambitious and striving so hard for more, not really happy with where you're at and wanting to improve in some way or another. I do think the key, however, lies in realizing how blessed you are, all of the time, and being able to recognize that and never lose sight of the why while striving for more.

Settling for more means learning how to be happy along the journey, even if/when the journey isn't exactly a happy one at that.

Settle for more, knowing that you deserve it.

Settle for more, knowing that you're worth it.

Settle for more, knowing that it's possible, and you have the power to make it happen (and others to help along the way!).

The difference between you and someone you envy is that you settled for less. Don't settle for less. Settle for more.

Have Some FUN Today

HAVE SOME FUN TODAY

The world can be a really sad, depressing place sometimes. When you turn on the news, it's either bad news or worse news—the good, sweet stuff rarely makes headlines, and if it does, it's on Good Morning America instead of the primetime slot. There's a heated political climate, there are terrorist groups, there are cheats, liars, and straight up evildoers. At the end of the day, it can be hard to hit the pillow feeling all good and cheery if you are actually aware of all of the nonsense and sadness and hardships that plague the globe today.

Then there's your own life. I know so many of you suffer from Type A-itis...#BeenThereDoneThat. We're perfectionists. We're workaholics. We're so serious about making it happen, sometimes at the expense of our own happiness. We have anxiety, we have fears and dreams, we have real life struggles. We have medical diagnoses and financial burdens and relationship stresses, and sometimes it's hard to hit the week with anything other than ugh.

So today, we're takin' it easy. We're taking a load off with something light-hearted, intentional, important, and FUN.

I'm about to give you PERMISSION—you ready for it?

Have some fun today.

For the longest time, my biggest problem wasn't that I wasn't hustling hard enough. I can always hustle hard enough. In the words of 50 Cent, I'm a hustler, baby!

My problem was an inability to let go and have fun without feeling guilty about it afterwards.

Have you felt the same? When you're at this stage of hustle and bustle, ambition and achievement, you sometimes don't know how to stop. When you're constantly go-go-go on the gas pedal, you don't know how to brake. It's all or nothing. You're either full steam ahead, neck deep in to-do lists and halfway to changing the world, or you're lying on the couch for six hours with Netflix and pizza. There is no in between. There is no balance.

It's not good, it is hard...and it needs work. It's also vitally important. Hustle hard and then have some fun today, because you deserve it, girlfriend!

We get super anal about our work. We get really tied into the grind. We forget to stop and think or eat and breathe sometimes, let alone have fun. Heck, if I had an additional cup of coffee for every one I've forgotten cold in the microwave, I'd never need Starbucks again.

But that's not healthy, good, or fun. Dude, what's a world without any fun?!

As perfectionists, we sometimes make the mistake of trying to define what is and is not deemed "acceptable" fun. The long-loved ideas of spontaneity and adventure that we long for and dream of in high school and college...they become replaced. They're replaced with a longing for accomplishment, advancement, and achievement, and we don't necessarily feel that fun and

career-furthering go hand in hand. There's not necessarily a place in our brains that fits both, comfortably, side by side, where we can reach important milestones in our lives while also having fun.

It's like society tells us to choose.

No, you can't be a boss and also have fun.

No, you can't have fun and also be a boss.

Fun and work cannot coexist. They come at the expense of the other.

You must choose.

I call BS. Have some fun today. Push the societal limits. You don't have to be a workaholic to do great things in work. You don't need to spend an entire day or night on leisure just to have a good time. You can actually have a bit of both, believe it or not. I swear to you, it's possible. It takes work and isn't always fun, but it is 100 percent possible to do something kickass today and have some fun today, too. You can do both. You might not be able to do both at the exact same time, and some days the balance might feel off, but it's important to never forget to have some fun today whether you're off writing a novel, training for a marathon, winning a Nobel Peace Prize, raising four kiddos, researching a thesis, or saving the world.

Important: There is no set metric for "fun." You define your own fun, and no one can tell you otherwise! As long as it makes you happy and smile and satisfies your heart and soul, it fits the bill. (If it's legal and safe, that's also a plus.) Don't judge your idea of fun, and don't compare it to others. Fun can be zip lining upside down over the jungle (#BeenThereDoneThat), or finally finishing a TV series that you've watched alone with your cats for eight Friday nights straight (#BeenThereDoneThatToo). Whether your "fun" is active, chill, with the squad, or flyin' solo, it's yours and yours alone so embrace it and make it count.

Also Important: You don't need a set amount of time for fun. Sure, a whole afternoon to kill sounds amazing (and sure as heck sounds fun). But for those who are trying to balance boss status and fun, whether you're the boss of a household or the boss of a Fortune 500 company, ain't nobody got time for a whole day of break! If you only have a few minutes to steal between everything you're juggling, that's fine! Just make 'em count. Savor them. Do something that you really really, really, REALLY want to do, just for you, just for fun. Don't compare the amount of time you have to others—it's not about that. It's never about that. It's about you and your own ability and willingness to have actual, real fun today.

AND LASTLY, the best way to live life: learn how to make the mundane fun. If you commute, take it as an opportunity to have fun via new podcasts, books on tape, new music, and only let yourself have fun with those things on your commute to really give yourself something to happily antic-ipate every weekday. Add little things to your workspace for a fun moment when you need a breather, like a candle or candle warmer, photos of fun memories, fun and inspiring quotes, etc. Have an inbox solely reserved for fun, to weed out junk mail and

promotional spam in one email, and the
good stuff in another. Sign up for words
of the day, quotes of the day, jokes of the
day—anything and everything fun, uplift-
ing, inspirational, and good to start every
day off right, and to look to when moments
get tough or tiresome.

Whether you have five minutes or five
hours, you can have some fun today.

CHECK-IN!

1. How have you been making time for yourself?

2. How will you better prioritize what's most important to you?

3. What's something that needs more of your intentional time, and what's another thing that needs more GRACE for the journey?

say
NO

SAY NO

Ever struggle saying no? I don't blame you. Google serves up over 3.5 billion ways to say no in 0.46 seconds, so clearly, you're not alone. We live in this age of YES.

Say yes to new opportunities!

I just said yes to everything when I was starting out!

This is the year of saying YES to myself!

Yes, yes, yes, yes, yes! Yes, sometimes saying yes is good. Sometimes it's good and necessary. Sometimes, though, *saying yes is unhealthy.* Sometimes saying yes means we're inadvertently hurting ourselves, or going BACKWARDS in our personal progress or productivity. Especially once we realize how stinkin' *sacred* time is, it becomes even more important for us to be able to maximize it, utilize it, and capitalize on it in our efforts to be our best damn selves as much as possible.

Listen, is anyone else so totally OVER saying yes to everything??? Really, it's exhausting. Instead, we should be learning to say. . .no.

I was talking with one of my girlfriends who was having the *hardest* time saying no to pretty much anything and everything. She was afraid of "hurting" her work by saying no, she was afraid of "hurting" her relationships by saying no…and the only thing hurting was herself, as she confessed feeling totally overwhelmed and overworked. Saying yes too much led to this fear and inability to actually say no without feeling a pang of guilt. She was being pulled in too many directions to count, forced to prioritize other people over herself simply because there weren't enough hours in the day to actually get done everything she had said yes to for others.

No bueno.

She struggles so much with the word no because it comes with full fear that the listener will revolt on the relationship.

The issue: Saying yes to others doesn't

mean you're also saying yes to yourself. And saying yes to others also doesn't mean you're truly helping them, at the end of the day.

Sure, saying yes to start might be "an opportunity," but when does an opportunity become something less than? I would see this happen in blogging all the time, in the world of "influencer marketing." Girls would "say yes" to that first sponsored "opportunity" of a brand wanting hours upon hours of their time and hard work in exchange for a bottle of shampoo or a $40 sweater. But one yes turns into another… and sooner or later, she'd find herself totally overworked and underpaid, not even sure what the heck her value even IS since her "yes'" were taken advantage of by those who sought it. (*Hint: That was me a few years ago.*) In my 6-plus years of blogging, I have NEVER had a disrespectful "opportunity" turn into a respectful one down the road. If someone wants you to say yes to something that purely and selfishly benefits them

alone, chances are, there won't come a time when those tides change.

Saying yes to others doesn't mean you're also saying yes to yourself.

In something like parenting, this isn't a bad thing—it's an essential. Raising little humans is a selfless gig, and it's not one where saying no for the sake of your own time is realistic. Saying no *does* of course come into play other times though—like when your kid reaaaaally wants more candy or an iPhone at age eight. Sometimes, you've gotta "be the bad guy" and say no, for your good AND their good, too. In that moment, somehow we can all understand and deal with that pang of disappointing someone knowing that at the end of the day, it's for our sanity AND their own good too, to hear the word "no." Which brings us to…

Saying yes to others also doesn't mean you're truly helping them.

We're people pleasers by nature and HATE the idea of disappointing others. BUT. Saying yes just for the sake of not saying no doesn't mean that you're actually saying YES—*you're just not saying no*. This was my friend's predicament: she came to the realization that she was saying yes to folks because they wanted something, but she didn't think what she was giving them was actually HELPING them. So it was a double whammy: say yes and give them what they WANT so that they feel happy in the moment, or say no and give them what they NEED and risk them being upset. She felt overworked, used, AND badly for prioritizing want over need and not having that harder conversation.

We say yes because we're afraid to say no, but what if saying no would be the more helpful answer for you AND for them?

If the girl in the cubicle next to you asks for help on a project but you feel just as confused, what good is your help to her at the end of the day? Your coworker is now dependent on you to help her get it done, and she doesn't actually know how to do it herself since she wasn't forced to figure it out; she's just banking on you. The hard truth might be that you're just not the best person to help on that job in particular, and that's okay! Saying no in that instance would benefit you AND your coworker by giving her the opportunity to a) learn it for herself, or b) find better help who might actually *be of help*.

SAY NO.

If someone asks you out on a date, what good is saying yes when you have zero interest or chemistry? Sure, in the moment they might feel good about landing a date, but sooner or later, you're going to HAVE to say no, lest you marry them. HA. Saying no would save BOTH of you the time and energy and allow you each to better spend that time finding your actual soulmates. SAY NO.

Feel no need to justify. Feel no need to explain. Feel no need to make up for it later.

Understand that "no" is a complete sentence, and your own sanity and well-being come first. Granted, it's a fine line fo' sho'. Saying yes to ourselves 24/7 would be selfish—of COURSE we want to rightly prioritize others when the time calls for it. But if something is jeopardizing your own mental health (or physical/emotional health), it might be a reaaaaally good time to say no. Ask yourself…

Will/would this bring me joy if I say yes?

Will saying no truly *hurt* me in some way? If so, is that a healthy and valid concern, or is it more of a concern that it wouldn't feel acceptable to say no in this instance?

Will this feel worth it to me?

Will I feel taken advantage of or used if I say yes?

Am I saying yes just because I'm afraid to say no?

SAY NO to things that don't bring true joy.

SAY NO when you have that gut feeling that something isn't just right.

SAY NO if you think it won't be fully worth your time or investment.

SAY NO so that you have more room to say yes.

I once heard Ashton Kutcher say something great about checking email; he said you've gotta start your day withOUT your inbox. Make your own to-do list, and don't let yourself check email until at least an hour or two has passed. Why? Because *your inbox is other people's to-do list for you*—it's not your to-do list for yourself. Chances are, you'll pop on Gmail and find yourself in a black hole for the next few hours, tackling other people's requests and demands as they come. Our days are short; our time is precious. Every choice is a yes or no that leads us closer or farther away from growing into our best selves. You'll feel more empowered and content in your own life when you feel comfortable confidently and kindly saying "no" when you know you need to or should. Saying yes to one thing means you'll have to say no to another thing. Make sure you're saying yes to things that you're A-okay accepting *over* other things, because you just never know when the next YES-worthy opportunity will come your way.

"Focusing is about saying no." –Steve Jobs

"Sometimes we need to say no, so we have more time to say yes." –Suzette Hinton

"Half of the troubles of this life can be traced to saying yes too quickly and not saying *no* soon enough." –Josh Billings

"Saying no can be the ultimate self-care." –Claudia Black

"*No* is a complete sentence, and so often we forget that." –Susan Gregg

"You can be a good person with a kind heart and still say no." –Lori Deschene

"The difference between successful people and really successful people is that really successful people say no to almost everything." –Warren Buffet

"What you don't do determines what you can do." –Tim Ferriss

Guaranteed you will feel a weight leave your shoulders.

BE KIND TODAY

One time in church, the sweet old lady in front of me turned around, put her hand on top of mine, looked me square in the eye and so warmly said, "You have a beautiful voice."

One summer, my intern, Sarah, and I were in the drive-thru line at Panera Bread for the usual grub when the guy said, "I threw in two cookies for you girls just because."

You know what this world needs a whooooooole lot more of, like, yesterday? Kindness. Not just the kindness that comes in the form of a Pinterest-ready kindness quote or double-tap-worthy Instagram caption. Real, hard, genuine, wholehearted kindness. The effort kind. The kind that is oh so needed today, tomorrow, and the rest of forever. The kind that neither requires nor expects anything in return.

The lady in front of me in church didn't have to give me a compliment. She could've gone about her day as normal, thinking whatever she would about my singing voice without sharing kind words.

The Panera worker could've just taken our money and given us our salads and bagels in the usual lunch hour rush. He could've carried out a transaction, gotten paid, and gone home.

But she didn't and he didn't. Both went out of their way to be kind. In doing so, it completely made my entire day (and week), having the potential to spark a whole slew of kind acts in return.

Be kind today.

It's easy to think of hypothetical situations that would warrant our kindness in the future. Times when we predict it'll be good and "worth it" to be kind, or times when a random act of kindness as seen on BuzzFeed would be fitting to DIY ourselves. But as good ol' Ralph Waldo Emerson once said, "You cannot do a kindness too soon, for you never know how soon it will be too late."

Be kind today.

The world is a sh*tshow sometimes, folks. It just is. It's way too easy to turn on the news, flip open a paper, or hop on Twitter and be bombarded by negative press after even more negative press. People dying, killing, hating, and spreading hurt. Unfortunately, the good stuff gets not nearly enough attention. So we're left wondering…is the world just a mean, cold place? Is kindness a dying breed?

I refuse to believe it.

As cliché as it might feel, if we want the world to actually be a happier, lovelier, kinder place for our kids and their kids' generations, it absolutely has to start with us. And it can start today.

Be kind today.

It's too easy to assume the worst, and when we assume the worst, we act the worst.

The cashier seems unfriendly and forgets your change? How rude—how did they even get this job?!

Someone cuts you off in traffic? What an ass; I hope he gets what's coming to him.

Your three o'clock client meeting is late and arrives only to look right through you? Doesn't she respect my time? I'll never refer her to anyone!

When in reality…

The seemingly terrible cashier's dog is sick, and her coffee shop paycheck isn't enough to pay for vet bills.

The seemingly reckless driver just got a call that his first baby is about to be born early, and he's trying to get to the hospital.

The seemingly thoughtless client is having major problems at home, and she's afraid her husband is being unfaithful— she's heading home after work for a hard conversation ahead.

We judge assuming the worst—why not assume the best? Judgments can be harsh, or they can be kind. Yes, sometimes a kind judgment may be given in an "undeserving" situation (i.e. the too-fast driver was really just being an idiot for no reason). But either way, your own mood and day will be better simply because you chose to be kind today for others.

If you're sittin' there like HECK YEAH, today's the day! I'm going to be kind! Here are 10 random acts of kindness to wet your whistle.

Strive to genuinely compliment three people in your day. Whether it's their singing voice or their shoes or their haircut or their sweet disposition, be kind today.

Pay it forward at the coffee shop. Whether that means paying for the person in line behind you, or telling the cashier to use the cash as a "wild card" to make a random person's day, be kind today.

Call someone up who has made an impact on your life but hasn't heard it lately. Whether it was an old friend from high school or a mentor at work, be kind today.

If the lady behind you at the grocery store seems to be in a hurry, offer her your spot in line. Whether or not her hurry is "worth it," be kind today.

Buy a bouquet of flowers and walk around the mall handing them out to unsuspecting strangers going about their regular shopping. Whether or not they think it's weird in the moment, they'll smile seeing that flower in a vase in their home, and it might be the only time they ever receive a flower from someone else, so be kind today.

Make a food basket for a family you know, in your church or neighborhood or school community, just because sometimes coming home from a long day at work to make dinner for five is really, really tiring. Whether or not your casserole recipe is up to par, be kind today.

Sneak a Post-It note into your neighbor's mailbox with an encouraging, anonymous note amidst bills and junk mail. Whether or not they know it's from you, be kind today.

For the animal lovers in the house, check out your local adoption shelter and find out their adoption fee to take home a dog or cat. Leave the exact amount (if you can) for an adoption, and instruct them to use it for a sweet family that comes in looking to adopt a puppy or kitty. Whether you're a cat or dog person, be kind today.

The next time you pass a homeless person on the street asking for spare change for a meal, ask if you can buy him/her lunch.

Whether or not they actually want the money for food, be kind today.

At your next restaurant outing, over-tip your server, and ask for their manager; leave a great compliment. Whether or not service was excellent, be kind today.

"As cliché as it might feel, if we want the world to actually be a happier, lovelier, kinder place for our kids and their kids' generations, it absolutely has to start with Us."

#CAFFEINATEYOURSOUL

I CAN DO hard THINGS

I CAN DO HARD THINGS

What's your favorite four-letter-word?

Hey! Not that kinda word, Karen! We're talkin' a four-letter-word that gets waaaaay too much use, and it's just gotta go. That word?

Hard.

"Monday mornings are so hard."

"I'm not looking forward to it—it's going to be so hard!"

"I'll try, but it's hard."

Really? Girlfriend, since when can you not do hard things? I see you ambitiously starting a new business. I see you strongly breaking personal fitness goals. I see you gracefully killing harsh words with kindness. I see you turning down a donut for a kale salad (you have more strength than me—ha!).

You can do hard things. You've just gotta believe that too. When you feel like you're between a rock and a hard place, remember that that "hard place" is only as hard as you allow it to be.

Whether or not something is "hard" is a pinch of truth, a dash of actual physical challenge, and approximately 94 percent mental game. There's obviously not some overarching qualifier for whether or not things are "hard." Writing a book is "hard" to some; others have hundreds of publications under their name. Running a marathon is a "hard" feat for many; others think it's "hard" to run one mile without stopping. Simone Biles' gold medal-winning routines are "hard" to every other gymnast on the planet…except Simone Biles. Whatever constitutes "hard" is almost entirely subjective, depending solely on your own interpretation of the word.

So why is anything "hard" for you?

If you truly want to live a limitless life, why do you constantly throw limitations on yourself, writing your own abilities and strengths off before you're even in the ring? Because it's "hard?"

I know why. It's because sometimes, you really don't believe you can do hard things.

Girlfriend, I gotta tell ya something.

YOU CAN DO HARD THINGS.

When was the last time you put your 100 percent effort into something "hard" and fell flat on your face? If you're jumping outta your seat now going, "ALL THE TIME, Erica! All the time, I'm a big failure and I try so hard but I always fail, I can't do hard things!" I need you to ask yourself a "hard" question:

But did you really give it all you've got?

Was there ANYWHERE in the picture, looking back, that could've used some improvement, extra effort, additional resources, added oomph…better mindset?

Chances are, when something is oh so "hard," we don't even give it all of our effort because we've already psyched ourselves out of the game. We've already written a little excuse sheet for ourselves—a permission slip to fall short. Our own potential is stunted right off the bat because we don't believe in our heart of hearts that we can do hard things.

Girlfriend, I so desperately want you to believe in yourself—in your own capabilities, in your own dreams, in your own everything. Because dang it, you can do hard things! You've already DONE hard things. You've confronted a coworker, you've birthed four babies, you've said goodbye to people you love, you've delivered bad news, you've buried beloved pets, you've battled freaking CANCER—you've done hard things in your life already, of that I'm sure.

If you have a pulse and you have a dream, you are no different from any other great anyone who has done anything "hard."

The key? Redefining "hard."

Some see "hard" as "impossible." But impossible says, "I'm possible!" Hard doesn't mean impossible—it just means challenging, new, out of your comfort zone. Time to get comfortable being uncomfortable and buckle up, because if you're going to grow and learn and actually do the impossible, you've gotta believe that you can do hard things.

This is it—you now have permission to do the "hard" thing that you weren't going to really do.

Go get in front of the mirror. Look yourself in the eye, and convince yourself: "I can do hard things."

I can do hard things.

Can you? (Yes, you can!)

JUST

Focus

AND

KEEP

Aiming

JUST FOCUS AND KEEP AIMING

I'm really digging arrows lately. Maybe that sounds totally hippy dippy and way too I-haven't-had-my-morning-coffee-yet, but hear me out. The symbolism behind arrows just rocks my world, and I can't think of a better way to literally fly into this week. You know what they say about arrows, right? An arrow can only be shot by pulling it backward. So when life is dragging you back with difficulties, you're being prepared to launch into something great. So, just focus, and keep aiming.

Sometimes, we hold ourselves back.

WHOA, what?

Yeah, I said it! I'll say it again for the folks in the back.

Sometimes, we hold ourselves back.

Ever play the What If game?

I'm sure you have. If you haven't, you're either Beyoncé or Jesus. We find ourselves in the "What If" zone, where there are, like, five different imaginary outcomes, none of which are ideal and none of which

are realistically all that plausible. Usually, that zone just consists of our fears that, nine times out of 10, don't come true.

Mondays can be tough because they're full of the week's "What Ifs." I used to start the day just feeling straight up nauseous at the thought of Monday morning. When I was in school, I'd run to my then-boyfriend and my momma feeling like one setback— or a few—would mean no job for me after graduation. One setback in a relationship would mean the friendship would never work long-term. One setback in blogging? I'd probably never reach my goals anyway, so I should just quit while ahead. Right?

Nope. No sir. Not right at all.

This brings me back to arrows.

Arrows literally only fly forward after being pulled backwards. It's basic physics here people—throwin' it back to AP Physics way back in high school. Whether you like to think of yourself as the archer or the arrow, you won't always hit the bullseye.

Sometimes you'll come so stinkin' close, and sometimes, you'll completely miss the target and you'll get a dart stuck in your parent's basement drywall (sorry, Dad). Either way, you pick up your dart or your arrow, and you try again. You're going to be pulled back time and time again, but with time and practice, you'll get there. You'll regain focus, you'll get more clarity, you'll hone your craft, and you'll aim higher and stronger and fiercer than you have ever aimed before.

While not every success story comes with an accompanying tale of extreme hardship or difficulty, many do. So on this Monday, wherever you may be and with whatever flavor coffee is floatin' your boat, I want you to remember this:

It took Henry Ford being completely broke five times before Ford Motor Company.

It took R.H. Macy seven failed businesses before NYC's Macy's.

It took JK Rowling 12 publishing houses before *Harry Potter and the Sorcerer's Stone*.

It took Thomas Edison nearly 10,000 tries before the light bulb.

Whatever your difficulty and whatever your stress, let this week be a reminder of all the amazing things you can do by just honing your focus and aiming higher towards greatness. You can—and you will—fly.

"An arrow can only be shot by pulling it backward. So when life is dragging you back with difficulties, you're being prepared to launch into something great."

#CAFFEINATEYOURSOUL

I AM ENOUGH

Confession time: For years, I STRUGGLED.

I was struggling, and no one knew. My struggle was one that I'd bet you've struggled with too, at one point or another, in one arena or another.

I wasn't enough.

Or rather, I didn't FEEL enough. Because feelings aren't facts.

Feeling: You don't feel enough. Fact: You ARE enough.

I am enough.

This all slammed me in the face one day, when I woke up just in tears. I had been feeling the weight of that week, and it was particularly heavy. There was an inbox full of demands, a sink full of dishes, a to-do list from here to Canada…and I hit a wall. So I woke up and just cried, feeling really small and inadequate and wanting relief from a multiplicity of things. (Shout-out to my 12th grade art history teacher for instilling "multiplicity" into my vocabulary.)

I thought to myself, How on God's green earth am I going to get everything done that I need to get done? Some might say "prioritize," but it was at the point where everything truly did need to get done, because due dates exist and I ran out of paper plates. I thought, Hey, since I'm not Superwoman or Beyoncé, I clearly don't have enough hours in a day to be a shining superstar. Something's gotta give, right? But here's the thing.

Our 24 hours are not the same as Beyoncé's.

I mean, Beyoncé has a total of eight nannies for her three children. If you're a fellow mama, I want you to read that sentence again. There's her, Jay-Z, and eight nannies. If you're a stay-at-home mama of three kiddos, you might be devoting your sole 24 hours entirely to your three musketeer rugrats. I mean, parenting ain't no joke, yo! But if you're Beyoncé, and a total of 10 grown-ups are caring for your children—that's a total of 240 hours in a day.

240 hours in a day—and that's just talkin' childcare! (They also have 24/7 nursing staff, and three bodyguards to drive Blue Ivy to school—talk about a pickup line!) Queen Bey has other household staff too, and an entire team for the business/music side of life.

Your 24 hours are not the same as Beyoncé's.

You are doing the best you can with what you have, to get closer to your best self.

You are enough.

Simple as that. Even when I'm hot-messing my way through life, spilling coffee on a growing pile of papers, tripping over a growing pile of laundry, and getting toothpaste on my contact lens (true story), I'm still enough, just the way I am.

So are you. I am enough.

We all have those moments, those days, those years where we feel lackluster, tiny, insignificant, unimportant, insecure, or in pain. We feel like we just don't measure up to what society wants us to be, what our friends or family think we are, or—perhaps even worse—what we strive to be ourselves. So let this be a personal shout out to any and all of you who have ever felt like you just weren't enough.

You are.

You were handcrafted fearfully and wonderfully in one helluvah spectacular image.

You are enough.

"You were handcrafted fearfully and wonderfully in one helluvah spectacular image. You are enough."

#CAFFEINATEYOURSOUL

No Rain,
No Flowers

NO RAIN, NO FLOWERS

On December 1st, 2018, I got the best Instagram DM maybe ever.

It said: "8/8/2016...you wrote a blog. No rain, no flowers. A million thank yous for that…"

Then, this chick proceeded to send me a picture of a tattoo that she got after reading this very mantra on my blog. A FREAKING TATTOO! I mean, "have someone get a tattoo from your writing" was right up there with "make out with Zac Efron" and "adopt 10 cats," and I didn't even know it.

No pressure or anything, right?

I digress.

Watching grass grow might be a total snooze-fest, but watching flowers grow is a whole new world. Blossoming is a beautiful thing. We see these totally insubstantial little seeds start off as nothingness, just packed with potential. Then we watch them slowly but surely open up to the world, soak up goodness, and grow, grow, grow. An exact metaphor for us, as we grow through what we go through.

But growth can be hard.

With growth comes growing pains—the tensions we feel as our bodies and minds evolve into something new, something better. But "better" doesn't always mean easier. Better can sometimes mean that life sucks a bit before better happens. The "suck" in life can feel like a total storm, where we're left soaking wet...and not in a romanticized Ryan-Gosling-and-Rachel-Adams kinda way.

When it rains, it pours amiright?

For those of us who love a good rain shower, a solid storm is rejuvenating. I couldn't love more the sound of rain splashing against my window, thunder rolling, and the occasional flash of lightning to brighten up the sky. To me, it's soothing and rehydrating to my literal soul, and I'm either taken to snuggling in bed a little longer, or I'm zapped with energy and get newfound fuel to hustle. I'm sure my other rain-lovers would agree—ain't nobody got time for lame rain. Light drizzle? Annoying. Quick shower? Awkward. If it's gonna rain, it better rain.

But we don't necessarily let the metaphor translate over to our own lives, and we're seriously missing out because of it. When we experience "rain" on our daily parades, it's too easy to let that little storm—no matter how short or small—completely throw off our day. Instead of letting it come and go like a mid-afternoon spring shower, we harbor on it in our minds and devote all of our energy into complaining about it, hating it, or wishing it never existed. We are derailed too easily, and suddenly a little sprinkling is a thunderstorm on our productivity and mood.

There are two people in life: people who love rain, and people who despise it.

Those who love rain embrace challenges, struggles, and perceived obstacles as opportunity.

Those who hate rain see hardships, surprises, and unwelcome guests as bubble bursters.

Whichever side of the fence you're currently on, here's why you should love rain:

No rain, no flowers.

Flowers don't grow without rain—point blank period. There's no getting around the fact that they need good ol' H_2O from the sky to survive, let alone thrive. Flowers see rain as opportunity—a life-breathing opportunity at that. They can't control how little or how much comes; a big-ass hurricane would surely rip them right out from where they're planted. But they can't change their roots—they can only bloom and grow accordingly. So they don't stress about the what ifs and the size of the possible impending storm. They just do their thang and blossom. No rain, no flowers.

Why can't we be the same way?

I get it, I get it…we have brains and hearts, and flowers don't. Yadda yadda yadda. You'd think that would clue us in even sooner to the uselessness of stress and worry though, right? HA. Oh, humans.

When it rains, let it pour into you as means of cleansing and healing.

When the sky of LIFE rains down, open yourself up for growth.

When it storms, stay steadfast in your beliefs and in yourself and know that you are worth more than your self-doubts, and you are prepared to perform at a totally new level.

Because without rain, there are no flowers. No rain, no flowers.

When you want to see never-before-seen growth and progress in your life, you're going to have to get comfortable being uncomfortable and weather whatever unexpected downpours come your way. The weather channel can't predict everything, and sometimes they're blatantly wrong. Just because you don't know every single thing comin' your way doesn't mean you can't live a full, happy, thriving life. In fact, you need to live a full, happy, thriving life in spite of whatever hits you close to home. Remind yourself: no rain, no flowers.

That's the key to living a life that's coming up roses. Taking your own personal thorns and whatever other sh*t comes raining down, and turning it into something beautiful.

Can you do that? (I know you can.)

I am
worth more
than my
self-doubts

I AM WORTH MORE THAN MY SELF-DOUBTS

When Monday hits you like a sack of bricks, it can easily feel like the bricks are made of everything but sunshine and rainbows. When the entire week is looming in front of your face (or heck, just the day!), it looks and feels like a jam-packed schedule of busy. But, there's somehow still room for self-doubt.

We always make room for self-doubt.

Why the heck is that?

Half the time I don't even "have time" to finish my cup of coffee in one sitting, but I can always make time for self-deprecating, self-defeating self-doubt.

Why the heck is that?!

We can be so good at loving on other people, but sometimes we are so dang bad at loving on ourselves. We let self-doubt infiltrate our minds and make us question our own every move, always feeling not enough and never feeling satisfaction for our own hard work. It's as if somehow our self-doubts become worth more than ourselves. Enter, today's Monday Mantra.

Say it with me.

I am worth more than my self-doubts.

It's so easy to doubt ourselves. It's so easy to let our minds run wild with thoughts of "you'll never make it," "you can't do it," "she can, but not you." It's so easy to fall into the cyclical trap, poisoning our own minds with our own thoughts unleashed.

We doubt that we will be the exception to the rule.

We doubt that we are worthy of our own power, or that we are worthy of the greatness and potential within us. That we are worthy of bringing it into the sunshine for all to see.

We doubt that we have "what it takes to make it." What the heck does "making it" mean, anyways?

We doubt that we're talented enough or pretty enough or smart enough or whatever enough.

It's so so, so, SO damaging, and there are not enough Band-Aids or therapists in the world to undo the damage we inflict upon ourselves when we refuse to rise above self-doubt and power forward in our own greatness.

But dang it, you are enough.

I'll say it again for the folks in the back.

YOU ARE ENOUGH!

When will you finally believe that?

You are worth more than your self-doubts.

SO MUCH MORE. You are worth more than your doubts, depression, and fears. You are worth more than your anxiety, excuses, and inner demons. You are simply worth more, point blank period. It's high time you believe it.

If you still don't believe it, call your best friend, memorize a Bible verse, and go take a walk around the block before coming back and re-reading this whole shebang, start to finish, all over again. You are worth more than your self-doubts. Believe it.

There are so many people in your life that you refuse to give up on—that you would refuse to quit with, regardless of what hardships or struggles come to pass. You have it in your head that these people are worth it, and that you will go the distance to ensure that you have the best possible relationship, no matter what human imperfections exist. Why don't you give yourself that same grace? Why do you refuse to give up on the best people in your life, but you're quick to quit when it comes to your "too big" dreams or deepest desires? You're willing to make sacrifices for the people you love…why don't you make more sacrifices for your dreams?

You doubt that you have what it takes.

You doubt that you are worth it.

You doubt that it will "pay off" somehow, and you're afraid of being selfish and having your own inadequacies and shortcomings slamming you in the face. Like, "HA, told ya you weren't good enough! Told ya you couldn't do it! Told ya she is better than you!"

Honey, that's just the devil talkin'. The devil is getting in your head, you're filled with fear, and you start to doubt every single ounce of goodness that you KNOW in the pit of your soul you bring to this good green earth.

But you know what?

You are worth more than your self-doubts.

When the doubts start swimming and you begin to think you just don't have what it takes, I need you to pause.

I need you to pause and breathe and remember this mantra. Look in the mirror and study yourself. Study the lines in your face, and remember all of the hardships you've faced and OVERCOME to put any stress lines there. Look in the mirror and see the glimmer in your eyes. This glimmer is the unstoppable force of passion and purpose in your heart, and it is meant to be out there for the whole damn world. Look in the mirror and say to yourself:

I am worth more than my self-doubts.

Then repeat it. Fifteen times. Staring at yourself in the face, and don't you dare look away. Don't stop until you truly believe it. Believe it, because you are worth it. You really, really are. Stop doubting everything that God has put in your heart. Stop doubting the amazingness that you've worked your entire life to create. You are worth it. You are worth more.

It's time you stop doubting that and truly believe it.

do less, RECEIVE MORE

DO LESS, RECEIVE MORE

Do you ever wake up, heart already beating fast with that sinking feeling of weight on your chest as your brain runs over your day's to-do list? You don't even make it to the Keurig and you're feeling stressed and irritable and less than stoked to start the day, because it's just so much on your daily plate.

Maybe you've just got an exceptionally cray cray schedule today, maybe you're a chronically anxious person, or maybe you're close to burnout.

Either way, it's way too easy in today's "hustle harder" society to feel more inclined to do MORE rather than do LESS. If you have dreams and goals you want to accomplish, society says GO GO GO! Faster, harder, smarter, longer…more! There are two ends of the spectrum. 1) Hustle hard and don't stop. If you're resting, you're doing it wrong, you're missing out on money, you're not reaching goals, you're falling short. 2) Fake a fever to spend a sick day binging a new Netflix release in pajamas with a box of pizza and a bottle of wine.

It's overwhelming.

Which brings us to this: "Do less, receive more."

Before diving in, let's get a few things straight. This doesn't mean slack off, nor does it imply you should just piggyback your way through life on other's successes and efforts. No way, José.

It means there's an order of operations, if you will—a checklist to follow in order to maximize your time, minimize your stress, and make the most out of everything you do.

We beat ourselves up every time we don't get through an entire to-do list. We feel like failures anytime we see someone on Instagram living a more glamorous life on seemingly less hustle. We battle feelings of total suffocation when we get to drowning-level and we fear we'll lose our minds altogether under the surface of the stresses and anxieties and doubts of our everyday realities.

We're doing so damn much. We're trying so damn hard. We're working so damn often, and we're not seeing any sort of "payoff"—no return on the investment.

So we're sent spiraling in panic and self-loathing, the dream diminishing to just that—a dream—instead of feeling like an attainable thing.

But we're doing too much.

We're spending so much time trying to play catch up in our own lives, that we're falling behind. We're burning out. We're falling short on all accounts. Instead of constantly looking to do MORE, it's due time we step back and do LESS—only with more focus.

We're not getting through whole to-do lists because the list is jam-packed with things that don't even fit within the time blocks of our day. We're judging ourselves based on other people's Instagram profiles, forgetting that pictures speak a thousand words and none of them show the FULL picture. We're consumed by stress because we're not sure what the heck to focus on, so we focus on EVERYTHING and it all carries weight.

But when you do less with more focus, you open yourself up to receiving more out of life in every regard.

Instead of trying to "do it all" à la Superwoman, remember that Superwoman didn't actually do it all. Her powers always wore off after 24 hours. She could "do it all" for a while, but it was literally impossible to be super forever. Remember, even Superwoman needed time to recharge. Everyone needs time to regroup, rejuvenate, and remember your WHY.

The next time you feel overwhelmed and need a breather from life, get in front of your mirror and give yourself a good look. See your furrowed brow, your frazzled face, your wigged out look of burnout, and remind yourself that you don't need to be like that. You are enough, just as you are, and you can be more by doing less.

Give yourself a gentle reminder, right in your own eyes:

I don't have to do it all at one time.

Even Superwoman didn't do it all.

I am enough, just as I am.

I can be more by doing less.

I do not need to stress, worry, or panic over what-ifs.

I can create my best life without sacrificing myself.

I give myself grace to do less and receive more.

I can focus more on less for better end results all around.

I am open to doing less, and I am open to receiving more.

I don't have to do it all at one time.

When you vow to do LESS, you're enabling yourself to dive deeper with a more pinpointed focus. Your mind isn't scrambling to fit it all in at one time anymore. Instead of half-heartedly, haphazardly doing 15 things, you can do five things better, smarter, more carefully than before. You become better at remembering things, better at prioritizing your time, and better equipped to really perform at your best.

Because of that, you're open to receiving more. You're setting yourself up to receive more goodness, because you are more intentional with the good that you're giving to others and the world. Instead of always looking for more, looking for less helps you set apart what really matters in your life, versus what you feel like you "have to" do for whatever reason. It's clarifying, rejuvenating, and freeing.

Do less, receive more.

I DON'T
try
I DO

I DON'T TRY, I DO

"Try" is an awful word, really.

"I'll TRY to do better." "I'll TRY to make it." "I'll TRY to think of a better solution." "I'll TRY to get up earlier." "I'll TRY to quit smoking, get a new job, finish my to-do list…"

The list goes on and doesn't stop anytime soon.

Here's the thing: TRY is just another word for "I can't."

Let that sink in for a hot sec.

"Try" is just another word for "I can't," because it's an immediate excuse for when we fail at what we've said we'll "try." When we we're going to try at something, there's an underlying assumption that we're not going to succeed. If you truly believed in yourself actually doing whatever it is you're "trying" to do, you wouldn't say, "Well, I'll try."

You'd say, "No problem…I'll do it."

I'll DO.

This brings us to today's mantra, which

I need you to repeat three times to yourself right now: I don't try. I DO.

Go ahead—repeat it again in front of the mirror while you're at it. I know we don't know each other like that yet, but girlfriend, I KNOW that you're a doer—you've got passion and skills and knowledge and heart, and you're going amazing places in life. You're also doing amazing things. Amidst hard times, challenges, struggles that you KNOW were so real, and people doubting you along the way (including yourself, since doubting yourself is like the common cold—we all catch that at some point), you still DID. That's the key here. So many things are going to pop up in your way. So many obstacles are going to try blocking your path. They're already trying to break you down, so if you just muster out a "try" in return? C'mon, I KNOW you're better than that!

Girlfriend, why do you doubt yourself? Why do you discredit your own strength?

Or on the flip side, why don't you just own up and commit already?

If you preface everything with "I'll try!" you're giving yourself an out. Maybe you're overcommitting yourself—a problem if you don't want to be 1) way overly stressed and stretched too thin and/or 2) seen as that flake amongst friends and peers who always needs to back out or change plans. Maybe you're trying to cover your own behind for the ol' "under-promise and over-deliver" tactic.

Maybe you doubt if you can actually do it or not, but you sure as heck don't know for sure unless you actually DO it. I heard someone say recently, "You don't 'try' in business. You're either doing a business or you're not." When you think about it—about what it really means to do something like launch a business—this statement couldn't be more true. To smartly launch something and set yourself up for success, there is no ROOM for "try." Heck, there's not even room to sleep or eat or breathe on a normal schedule half the time! Something as big as your own business is not a new food to test or pair of shoes to try on, so get in or get out!

DO or don't do.

Stop lying to yourself and others by "trying." You are worthier than that. Nix the "try" and just DO everything that you are capable of doing. Change "I'll try my best" to "I'll DO my best." When the spotlight is on you, there is no try—you just DO, and whatever happens happens, and the show must go on, and regardless of what happens on stage, you still take a bow at the end and life keeps happening.

Don't try. Just DO.

"If you truly believed in yourself actually doing whatever it is you're 'trying' to do, you wouldn't say, 'Well, I'll try.' You'd say, 'No problem. . .I'll do it.'"

#CAFFEINATEYOURSOUL

WHAT ARE YOU GONNA DO ABOUT IT?

WHAT ARE YOU GONNA DO ABOUT IT?

You know that friend who complains a lot?

At this point things might get awkward, if you are that friend.

Let's call her Negative Nancy. Nancy is...well, pretty darn negative. She's always coming to you with something that's wrong. Even worse, she's coming to you with things that are wrong, and she's got absolutely ZERO plans to change anything about her situation or environment to make it better.

"Karen at the office is SO annoying—she always expects me to get her work done for her."

"No matter what I do, I can't get to the gym. It's my husband's fault—he won't watch the baby!"

"My house is too small—our stuff is everywhere! I just wish we could afford a bigger place."

Whenever I'm on the receiving end of that sort of rant, I let it go.

I let her breathe. I validate her genuine concerns or struggles.

Then, I offer one question:

What are you gonna do about it?

Are you just gonna keep complaining? Or are you willing to listen to some advice, and act on it? Are you willing to DO something about your problem and get off the struggle bus?

. . .Or are you just looking for a fairy godmother to wave away your problems and hand you the perfect life?

I mean, y'all, this is tough. It can be TOUGH to admit when you're just wallowing in self-pity, or looking for an escape hatch, and avoiding the hard work altogether. That ain't cute, and it ain't comfortable, since it forces us to take a good, long, hard look in the mirror and confront any laziness or complacency staring back.

One of my best friends, Chelsie, battled and beat childhood cancer. She's a freaking warrior, and she taught me a lesson I'll never forget. She said, "You only have five minutes to be the victim."

You can bitch and moan and complain for FIVE MINUTES—set a timer. Once that timer beeps, you're done. No more venting, no more ranting, no more calling your best friend up in arms or texting the group chat in a panic. No more. Nada. You're donezo. At some point, you've gotta cut the useless crap (aka, complaining), and you've gotta DO something about it.

Karen at the office tries throwing work on you? Say no. You're not obligated to do someone else's job—you've got one of your own!

Can't get to the gym? No problem—pick up two dumbbells and a yoga mat on your next Target run. Your living room is now your gym.

Stuff is all over your house? Make a game out of it for your family next Saturday, and do a 15-minute speed clean. Everyone tidies up. Even better? Purge a few things that no longer serve you, and

your small space will feel bigger AND less cluttered.

Whatever you've been hoping and dreaming for can happen, but only if you DO something about it. Having dreams means diddly squat if you don't have the courage to bring them down from the clouds and onto this earth.

You might never feel ready. You might never feel sure. You might never feel completely stress-free or calm or worthy.

But you can still BE ready, and you can still BE worthy.

The next time you feel stuck in a rut, whether you feel behind in your professional goals or unmotivated in your personal goals or just overall BLAH, here are three action steps to get unstuck:

1) Identify why you're stuck. Why aren't you moving forward? Are you scared? Feel like you don't have the necessary skills or resources yet? Were you never really dedicated to it in the first place? First figuring out (and coming to terms with) the underlying reason why

you've hit pause is crucial to fully understanding the situation and being able to recommend a remedy.

2) Figure out one way to pivot from your "why." So you're scared…move past fear by figuring out one reason you should that trumps why you shouldn't. You don't have some important skills you'd need to move forward? Figure out one thing you can practice, do, or invest in that would earn you that skill. You didn't really care too much about achieving it in the first place? That's okay…now use this experience to choose a NEW goal that you actually care about.

3) Do something about it. You've figured out the why and a next step, so now what are you gonna do about it? Through every stage, the choice is yours. Do something about it. You are in control of your own life. When you wake up and feel crappy on a Monday morning, yes, you absolutely could hit snooze three (more) times and nearly miss clocking in on time. Yes, you absolutely could skip your workout, or ignore your chores, or miss your morning routine altogether.

But you've got one shot to be your best self—you've got one life. Sister, you've gotta show up. Not just for your boss or your family or friends, but for YOU. The more you subconsciously set your own mood and day backwards, the worse you'll feel later on, and it's all because of things you've done (or have not done) to bring you to that point. This doesn't just apply to goal-writing or to little everyday tasks. The same theory goes for BIG dreams. Like your dream to travel the world or start your own business. What are you gonna do about it? If you feel like you have no idea where to even begin on digesting those dreams, start with the three step process: figure out why you have no clue where to start. If you aren't sure how to begin thinking about launching your own business selling coffee mugs and stationery, maybe your first step involves Googling "how to start a business." See, you can do that! Maybe then, you watch a YouTube video on printing mugs from your garage. After that, you read a blog post that details creating an actual business plan, and you do some research on becoming an LLC. Baby steps, people! It just takes some action. So…what are you gonna DO about it?

"Whatever you've been hoping and dreaming for can happen, but only if you DO something about it. Having dreams means diddly squat if you don't have the courage to bring them down from the clouds and onto this earth."

#CAFFEINATEYOURSOUL

What Are You

waiting for?

WHAT ARE YOU WAITING FOR?

I'm gonna cut right to the chase: you are holding yourself back.

A few Mondays ago, we chatted about taking action steps towards your dreams and goals. Being able to say to yourself, "But what are you gonna DO about it?" and using that as a jumping-off point to outline your next steps, get pumped up, and all that jazz. But at the end of the day, drawing out your whole action plan from yesterday through the year 3000 won't make a damn difference if you're constantly stuck waiting for "the right moment" or "the right time" to come along and tap you on the shoulder.

It's not going to.

This isn't a cheesy "follow your dream!" fest—it's a legit question. When was the last time you figured out what you were going to DO about something and then just STARTED, right away or shortly thereafter? You have that inkling in the back of your brain and deep within your heart that just itches to chase after your true passion.

The spark is there, yet oftentimes, there's just something that we wait on, as if the universe needs to give us permission to live our best lives and be our best selves.

If you're waiting for permission, this is it.

You've got your goals in life; you've got your goals for today and tomorrow. You know what you hypothetically have to do to get started on them all, but maybe there's just something holding you back. There's something that seems to be standing in your way, even if you can't palpably feel or see what it is. You have to ask yourself: "What are you waiting for?"

Maybe it's a fear of failure, a fear of being rejected, a fear of disappointing yourself or others.

But you know what? Nothing gets accomplished if you don't get started. If you're constantly feeling paralyzed by inaction and fear of one thing or another, you have to know that you are holding yourself back from reaching your potential. YOU are.

Not your kids, not your husband, not your best friend or your worst enemy—YOU.

Even if you are scared—because dude, reaching out on a limb to pursue a dream is freaking terrifying sometimes!—I promise you, you HAVE to grab the dream by the horns and stop waiting around for it to fall out of the sky and into your lap. Scary, but necessary.

No one says you have to do it all in one day.

The point is to stop waiting, and start. There will rarely be a perfect time to start. How many times have you thought about what you really—and I mean really—want in life and immediately followed that thought with a "Yeah I can do that, but only when I have/do/accomplish _____."

Bull. Sh*t.

Cut the "yeah, but" out of your life now. You think you need more money, time, education, support…maybe a new suit and heels, or new hair, or new whatever. You know what you really need?

You need to cut the excuses.

You're making excuses and cheating yourself out of your own dream. Let go of excuses. What are you waiting for? Accept the challenges. Surround yourself with support. Work through the fears. Don't let them hold you back—you've got far too good of a life ahead to warrant unnecessary crap standing in your own way. What are you waiting for?

Often, the first steps are the hardest, but level of difficulty is not where we should aim our attention. Focus, instead, on one step at a time! Cliché, but that's literally how you learned to walk way back in the day when everything seemed way too big and loud and your biggest aspiration was to not crap your pants in public. If you can keep working towards your goals for today, and then tomorrow, you can do it again… just for one more day. Rinse and repeat.

What are you waiting for?

Before you know it, you will have gotten that degree, cleaned your house, earned a black belt, quit smoking, lost the weight, built that business—you name it. Take at least one small step in the direction of your dream. Today. HECK, THIS MORNING! Then, keep stepping.

Time is unforgiving. It moves forward no matter what we are doing or thinking or stressing over.

So we have to be forgiving to ourselves, and give that oh-so-necessary permission to pursue more.

Obstacles cannot keep you stuck when you can step higher. If you can't step higher over them, go under them, around them, THROUGH them if that's what it takes, girlfriend. But HANDLE THEM like the boss that you are with a big fat "What are you waiting for?"

Seriously though. What?

TODAY IS NO ORDINARY DAY

Today is no ordinary day! Whether it's the week of Christmas, your birthday, mid-April, or the end of a rainy Tuesday, every single day has the potential to be something more than ordinary. Dare I say…extraordinary. The only limits on the potential of any day are the ones that you set there all by yourself.

Yup. You are the one making your ordinary days ordinary.

Because you are the one in control of your own life. If you don't like something, for the most part, you can take solid steps towards changing it. Of course, some things are just blatantly out of our control—like the death of a loved one or a job layoff. Life throws a lot of unexpected sh*t our way sometimes. For many of us, though, we've got a pretty heavy hand in at least what direction our sails are set. When you see potential for improvement anywhere along the line, it's up to you to start making. It. Happen.

Because today is no ordinary day.

It's the day when you can finally decide to take control of your own life. It's the day you decide to conquer a fear, no matter how small (or big!) it seems. Today is when you finally take the plunge in trying a new hobby or uncovering a hidden talent. You can hit the gym to tackle that inevitable New Year's Resolution. Even better? You can nix the resolution all together and just do it, and then you can wake up again tomorrow (and the next day, and the next day…) and do it all over again. It's the day you finally tell your person how you feel about them, or the day you decide to sever a tie that you know deep down is just holding you back from your truest, best self. Today isn't ordinary because you only get this day once. You only get this moment once, no matter how cliché that may sound.

It's no ordinary day, because it's got "potential" written all over it. There's the potential to be something bigger than yourself—the potential to be extraordinary.

Another thing: "extraordinary" doesn't have to mean so-crazy-awesome-even-Beyoncé-would-be-proud. Nope. That's not realistic, or even humanly possible for many of us muggles. It just has to be something beyond your ordinary.

Something to make you feel good about yourself, so that at the end of the day, when your head hits the pillow, you feel good.

Make today yours.

"It's no ordinary day, because it's got 'potential' written all over it. There's the potential to be something bigger than yourself—the potential to be extraordinary.

#CAFFEINATEYOURSOUL

SUCCEED ON PURPOSE

SUCCEED ON PURPOSE

"Succeed on purpose."

Well, that's a no-brainer, right? Of COURSE you want to succeed, and you've got faith in yourself to know that if you succeed…hopefully it ain't an accident! But why do you want to succeed in the first place?

Let's back it up a step.

No matter your job, career, or day-to-day schedule, why do you want to "succeed" at whatever it is you do? Chances are, it's not just for the money you could make or the status or recognition you could have. It's probably something so much more than that—it's because it means bringing you closer to your true purpose in life. Maybe your success as a personal trainer comes from the high of watching people transform their bodies and minds for the better. Maybe your success as a parent comes from wanting your kids to see a better life than you had growing up. Maybe your success as a housecleaner comes from your passion for helping families regain a sense of clarity and calm in their physical space.

I 100 percent believe that your work needs to be completely fueled by your purpose. Now, before you jump on that, let me explain: I do think you can find purpose in even the most "mundane" jobs. Your purpose doesn't necessarily mean that you're absolutely obsessed with and overjoyed by the job you have—that's just not the case for many folks. But your purpose doesn't have to be this direct line correlation to the actual job you're doing or the career path you're currently on (i.e., if you're a resident at a hospital, your purpose might be to become a physician and save lives, but there's not necessarily a hierarchy for folks who drive the trash truck or work the McDonald's drive-thru. That's not saying there is ANYTHING wrong with those gigs; it just means that "purpose" might not look the same for everyone. Your purpose can very well be to just make enough money to feed your family, or to save up for a nice vacation someday, and that's A-okay.

Too often, people make important decisions that impact the rest of their lives based on what makes the most money or what other people are doing or what people seem to expect of them. Something may work out, but it's probably more likely going to lead you to burn out, unhappiness, and a lack of fulfillment in your career and life. That sense of unfulfillment will stem from the fact that deep down you still know whether or not you are being true to your purpose. No matter the external accolades, awards, or recognition, the voice inside your head and your heart still speaks the loudest. This has nothing to do with your deeper, underlying sense of self and reason for being. (Even if you're sitting there saying sister, what I'm doing right now is out of pure necessity and I don't have the luxury of thinking about my "purpose"—yes, you do!) You can wake up every day and do your best to make it through the nine-to-five without spilling coffee on yourself (guilty) or falling down stairs (guilty), but here's some truth:

You are better than that.

You have reason for being here. You have reason for being in the job you're in now, for doing what you're doing, for liking what you're liking, and thinking what you're thinking. There's a reason there, and in that, purpose and meaning.

Maybe your reason is making people smile when all they want to do is cry. Maybe your reason is being an unparalleled listener, the breadwinner for your family, or the bread-maker, always cooking really special meals. While you can say it's obvious to TRY every single day and put in effort and strive towards goals and forge your own path to success, it's equally important to make sure your successes align with your greater mission in life—that they mean something beyond that initial swell of joy and achievement.

When you get up every morning, you've got a choice to make. Choice number one: You can choose to meander through the day, mentally chasing the weekend (or at least your 3 p.m. Americano). Choice number two: You can choose to live out your purpose by intentionally dedicating every moment to reaching a deeper meaning and connection. Sure, you can't control every "success" or "failure," but if you're purposefully positioning yourself towards your own success, by golly you've got a better chance of reaching that than the alternative.

Now you're set on succeeding on purpose…but how the heck do you find your purpose in the first place?

Figure out the bottom line of what you love and why you do what you do. How do you like making people feel? What sorts of basic tasks or processes get you excited? Are you someone who loves looking at things in a more scientific light? Does writing really light you up? Do you really rock at getting and staying organized, or do you have a real knack for listening to other people's problems and helping them find solutions? Make a list of some things you love to do, and make a list of some things that you think you're pretty darn decent at (or could become decent at—we've all got potential!).

Once you figure out at the most basic level what really makes you feel like you're living your dream life, you're that much closer to making that dream life a reality. Sometimes you'll have more than one purpose in your life, and that's okay. Purpose can evolve and fluctuate as you grow and develop and ride out the bumps and curves that life throws at you, and that's all okay. Even when you're completely unsure what your purpose is, sometimes making decision after decision in the moment, embodying what you believe to be good and right, will end up pointing you towards your purpose after all. Create your own definition of success by unapologetically living out your every day with such vigor and intention, people wonder where the heck you got the drive.

Succeed on purpose. At the end of the day, we've got one life to live, as cheesy and cliché as that may be. You've got one life. You shouldn't be settling for anything less than what you are absolutely capable of achieving, doing, accomplishing. At the core, identify your purpose. Why are YOU on this earth? What makes YOU unique and special, and what can YOU bring to this world that will help another human being in some way or another?

Don't be afraid of success in your life. Embrace it and go after it like the last slice of pizza.

"Sure, you can't control every 'success' or 'failure,' but if you're purposefully positioning yourself towards your own success, by golly you've got a better chance of reaching that than the alternative."

#CAFFEINATEYOURSOUL

THE GRASS IS GREEN WHERE YOU WATER IT

THE GRASS IS GREEN WHERE YOU WATER IT

You know the drill: "The grass is always greener on the other side." I'm sure you've also heard by now (or at least seen on a Pinterest board somewhere down the line): "Comparison is the thief of joy." True and true.

You know what's sad? It's sad how quickly we surrender our own joy because we see someone else doing something different and we want their joy instead. This Monday Mantra can turn any gray Monday…green: The grass is green where you water it.

This means "the other side" isn't part of your equation. It can't be. Put your blinders on, and, as my ninth grade history teacher, Mrs. Morse, would've said, "Stop rubbernecking." Keep your eyes on your own paper, and stop the constant comparisons to everyone else and their mother when it comes to you doing your own job and what you love best.

If you live by the first not-so-great saying, "The grass is always greener on the other side," you're literally allowing for someone else to have a happier yard (and life) just because you can't see the already existent good in yours. Or, perhaps even worse, you're unwilling to put in the really hard work that's needed to get your own yard in tip-top shape.

It takes work.

If you want to live a kickass life, there's always going to be someone doing it better than you, but that's not the point because there's always someone out of the seven billion people on this planet that can do something better than you. It takes work, and sometimes that may be why we find it temporarily easier to just envy others and whine about why they have it so easy or why they just had success "handed to them." But what good is that in the long run? It gets us nowhere, and our grass is still burnt in the end.

Rise above that and water your own grass instead of looking over the fence at the neighbor's lawn. Get your tools out, get some knowledge, and get to breaking a sweat and earning your own success that you can—and will!—create for yourself.

If someone else's grass is green, it's because they're spending time at Home Depot wandering the garden section, figuring out the right fertilizers to put on it. They're not sitting on their bums staring out the window at your grass—they're putting in work to get their own grass as green as can be.

Sometimes plants have a dormant phase. It doesn't mean the plant is dead—it's just resting and readying for the next season of growth. All plants have root systems, including grass. You can't see it happening, but it's there, and it's essential to any sort of growth at all. People need roots, too— the core values and integrity that anchor you to who you are and keep you grounded (pun intended). They're the unchangeable pieces of you that all other things are built upon. In this society, instant gratification is a thing. Sometimes we give up and walk away too quickly because our own grass

isn't growing as fast as someone else's, or we just feel like we're not good enough to make it happen ourselves.

The lesson here?

By spending time worrying about and focusing on what everyone else's yard looks like (aka, their job, their relationships, their kids, their life), you're wasting time that could otherwise be spent on watering your own yard. The result is a whole lot less confidence in your own work, a whole lot more obsession with the world around you, and a whole lot less progress in your own yard.

Sometimes you need to push yourself to take the step, like forcing yourself to water your houseplant because it's starting to look like toast (guilty), because you still see the potential.

You have potential.

So nix the comparisons, keep working hard, and keep your eyes on your own yard.

CHECK-IN!

1. What is one limiting belief that you've been holding onto about yourself and about what you are capable of?

2. Where is an area or person in your life that you can (and will) say NO to more moving forward?

3. Have you been comparing your grass to someone else's instead of watering it? Where can you water it now?

FAIL FORWARD

Martha Stewart would ban me from her kitchen.

God bless my husband for being a dang good cook, and bless up to God for a husband that can cook when I just can't. He hath provideth. Because this girl? Not the sharpest knife in the kitchen.

My hubs makes a MEAN chicken noodle soup. It's an entire afternoon affair, and it's the kind of soup that warms the soul and makes for a week's worth of loaded Tupperware.

When I was in college and we were just dating, J thought it was a great idea to have me make the family's famous chicken noodle soup recipe while he was at work. I had Friday off from classes, so I thought THIS IS IT—I'm going to make the meanest chicken noodle soup on the planet, he'll be so impressed, he's going to want to marry me tomorrow.

I spent all day prepping this dang soup. I cleaned and chopped bags of carrots and celery, I cleaned a whole chicken by hand—I was in it to win it. But then Jamie came home, and apparently…not Martha Stewart, folks.

I hadn't taken the strings off of the chicken.

I put the noodles into the soup with everything else.

If you're a chef extraordinaire (or maybe if you've just made homemade soup before), you probably just winced, because you KNOW that ain't good. But in case you are like I was then, here's why that's a big fat no-no: the noodles turn to mush. You don't end up with chicken noodle soup—you end up with chicken mush soup. Needless to say, I royally screwed up the soup.

Especially thanks to social media, it's so easy to see others' successes and immediately reflect on our own personal triumphs—or lack thereof—and feel upset, unmotivated, and discouraged. I follow countless Instagram accounts who share

Pioneer Woman-worthy meals on fancy Mackenzie Childs dinnerware, and here I am dissolving pasta. I mean, OOF.

If we're talking about real women with real lives and real realities…y'all, sometimes we fail.

It's not even like a "Oh shucks, that was an oops" kind of thing.

It's a blatant failure.

It's an I-just-ruined-an-entire-week's-worth-of-food kind of failure, or much worse.

You had a goal, an instruction, a task, an assignment, and you completely missed the mark, falling short and not achieving what you were supposed to or what you thought you could.

It stinks. It stinks, it stings, and it could be embarrassing and hurt your self-esteem, possibly stifling your ambition in the moment, too—maybe causing you to go into existential crisis mode and question your whole purpose in life.

But when we fail, we need to fail forward.

Maybe I convinced myself this was the key in life after tripping one too many times on the sidewalk over my own two feet and falling on my face. "Hey, at least I'm a step farther than before!" But really, what good is there in constantly letting our shortcomings and "failures" get the best of us and keep us down on the ground? (Answer: No good at all.) No matter how hard you want to try and go back and make things different or "better," you get no re-do option. We know a few things here:

1) Worrying is useless. You can't change the past and you can't know the future, so stressing out about either is literally a lost cause.

2) Meditating on mistakes is the fastest way to make them happen again. Remember when you were a kid in a sports game or dance recital or some other performance? Even a tough test in school or speech, your coach or teacher most likely told you to envision how you wanted the exhibition to turn out. Research has proven that the surest way to set yourself up for great results is to literally sit and think

and imagine yourself going through all of the motions exactly as you want them to go down. Since meditating on the good things you want to happen is a good way to help make them happen, meditating on the bumps in the road will likely have a similar effect, and you probably don't want that to happen.

3) Sometimes, failures end up being blessings in disguise. Okay, I know I'm not alone here. How many times has something happened to you that you thought you'd never recover from, and then lo and behold, you do. Not only do you recover from it, but you come back stronger, smarter, more equipped to handle the next test in life, and it turns out that the "failure" was just a speed bump along the road?

We are all going to fail. Easier said than believed, but it's true—you're going to miss a deadline, the guy next to you isn't going to get the job, the teenager a few doors down is going to fail the driver's test (twice), and your best friend is going to break her daily SoulCycle pact, and they're going to feel like a failure for the good part of a month.

That's okay.

But staying back in that woe-is-me mode, wallowing in self-pity and meditating on the failures?

That's not okay.

When we stumble and fall—what some might call "fail"—we can't just get back up. We've gotta get back up and take a step forward.

Because failing forward is the only way to stumble upon progress and greatness.

GET
COMFORTABLE
BEING
UNCOMFORTABLE

What's more uncomfortable than a Monday? Maybe you slept in on Saturday, maybe you enjoyed relaxed family time on the couch after Sunday church, or hopped back into bed for a quick siesta, all comfy and cozy, and then BAM, HELLO MONDAY 6 A.M. ALARM. AKA...the opposite of comfy and cozy.

You know where else we like to stay comfy and cozy?

Comfort zones. We like our comfort zones like we like our beds—far too much sometimes. We all know the saying: with great risk comes great reward. It's time to chat, because it's due time that we get comfortable being a little bit uncomfortable in life.

We know when we're comfortable. Life feels good, complacent, easy, routine. It's a "can't complain" sort of lifestyle full of expected happenings, where unexpected happenings are handled in expected kind of ways. We don't like awkwardness or butterflies or nerves on the reg, because it can be hard. It's hard taking the first step towards something that feels so big, whether that's moving to a new city, starting a new job (or quitting your current one), ending a relationship, launching a business—even getting a new haircut or purging your closet.

The awkwardness and butterflies and nerves are hard because with them often comes fear, anxiety, and stress that it won't all work out. That it won't work the way you hope it does, that you're not ready, or that you somehow won't be able to handle whatever comes your way as a result.

But the way I see it (and Eleanor Roosevelt would probably agree with me) we should do something every day that's a little bit scary. Not scary like Insidious: Chapter 3, because that crap is just horrifying and ain't nobody got time to be scared pants-less, but scary in a way that gives you that feeling in your stomach that always appears right before you do something big. I don't mean literally big or universally big...I just mean big to you. Maybe it's giving a speech that you've spent hours perfecting, and you're afraid of public speaking. Maybe it's having the guts to cut off a relationship that you've been in a while, when you just know in your heart that it's not the right thing for you anymore. Maybe it's coming up with this seemingly crazy entrepreneurial idea that you're undeniably crazy passionate about, and having the chutzpah to make it happen. Or maybe it's cutting out your daily Starbucks on your commute and instead trying a new tea or green juice for a bit. It's leaving the comfortable behind.

I love this quote from Brian Tracy: "You can only grow if you are willing to feel awkward and uncomfortable when you try something new." Why? Because that's when you know that what you're trying is worthwhile. You're trying something that pushes you into new boundaries and helps you grow and blossom into your next, truest self. If you're forever waiting until you're "ready," you might never start.

We're all dynamic, evolutionary people in the sense that our bodies, thoughts, minds, personalities are constantly (hopefully) growing and changing. The experiences and information we gain and the people we meet work to mold us and change us and better us, as we continue on this quest towards being our personal best. If we want this change to happen readily, though, we have to be open to change. We have to be open to getting blatantly uncomfortable sometimes to push ourselves into new grounds and really grow. Don't those flutters in your gut let you know that you're onto something important?

When doors open, you have to be brave enough to walk through them. You have to be willing to leave a comfort zone behind in the dust and do things before "you're ready." Ready is just a state of mind, after all. It's a feeling—it's not a fact.

If I can't convince you to nix the comfort zone, maybe this can:

"When God calls us to step out of our comfort zone, He is not calling us to be comfortable in the situation. He is calling us to be comfortable in HIM in spite of the situation."

One last goody from Francis Chan: "But God doesn't call us to be comfortable. He calls us to trust Him so completely that we are unafraid to put ourselves in situations where we will be in trouble if He doesn't come through." Can I get an AMEN? Cheers to getting uncomfortable this week.

TAKE THE TIME

The only thing we all have is time, and often, it's the thing we take most for granted.

We spend time with friends, but we spend it on our phones. We figure we'll see people again, so we don't necessarily feel the urgency in really squeezing out every possible second together. Instead, we half-ass our way through get-togethers, intermittently checking notifications and refreshing inboxes in case something "important" comes up.

We forget that spending time with our friends and loved ones IS the important thing. Everything else can wait.

Really. It can.

In today's society, we're conditioned to believe that our notifications control us. An "urgent" email means we should stop everything else in life. Repeated phone calls mean it just can't wait. While sometimes this might totally be the case and something really can't wait, oftentimes…it can.

We take the time for things that we think matter in life, oftentimes forgetting that they're not necessarily what really matters in the long game.

In this go, go, go world of dinging phones and perpetual stimulation, don't forget to take the time.

Take the time. . .to spend—unplugged!—with friends. Put the phone down. Put the phone down in another room. Talk. Ask questions. Learn new things. Have deep conversations about things that matter to you.

Take the time…to journal. Write down words. Write down feelings. Get to know yourself repeatedly. You are always changing, always growing, always blossoming into your best self.

Take the time…to call your grandparents. Tell them you love them.

Take the time…to go on walks outside (also unplugged). Stop and smell the roses.

Take the time…to clean the house. The

whole house. No more shoving things under rugs or in closets.

Take the time…to identify what really matters to you. In life, in friendships, in work, in play. In future homes, in pairs of jeans, in liquid lipsticks, in cups of coffee.

Take the time…to learn something new. Something new to cook, or an instrument to play, or a new style to wear.

Take the time…to chat with neighbors. You might have really cool people all around you.

Take the time…to read a book, just because.

Take the time…to purge your life, of anything that no longer serves you or brings you joy.

Take the time…to call people. Instead of texting, pick up the phone, throw in headphones, and TALK. Have personal conversations instead of impersonal texted words. Hear someone's voice and get to know what really makes them LOL.

Take the time…to get organized. Loose papers, random knick-knacks, piles of clothes…organize it all.

Take the time…to pick up some candles from Bath & Body Works as soon as they're half off. Thank me later.

Take the time…to get one step closer to a really big dream. Write down the dream, work backwards, and figure out one thing—just ONE thing!—that you can do TODAY to bring you a bit closer to that finish line.

Take the time…to treat yo'self.

You say you don't have the same money as her or the same education as him, but you DO have the same time. Twenty-four hours, baby. Of course, what fills those 24 hours depends on so many things, and having extra help in certain areas is a privilege in helping exchange time in different ways.

Take the time to identify what matters most to you in life—where you want to be in a year, in five years, in 10. Then take the time to identify what matters most to you NOW—will it help steer your course

correctly to end up at the right final destination for the mile markers you just made?

You can "someday" yourself out of a
life. Make sure you take the time for what
matters most along the way.

OPPORTUNITY OR OBSTACLE?

"It's either an opportunity to grow, or an obstacle to keep you from growing."

As I was sipping some really, really good coffee, I came across this gem from Wayne Dyer and BOOM. That was it. The full quote is, "With everything that has happened to you, you can either feel sorry for yourself or treat what has happened as a gift. Everything is either an opportunity to grow or an obstacle to keep you from growing. You get to choose."

You get to choose!

Opportunity or obstacle?

The whole point of this whole Monday Mantra thing is because Mondays can be hard for many of us muggles. Every Monday is a new week that's dawning, whether you feel ready or not, and you've got two options: you can rise to the occasion, carpe diem, and grow; or you can stay in bed a bit too long, drown yourself in espresso, and spend all day complaining about how Monday is—surprise!—here again and the weekend is gone and it's gonna be a long week and there's so much to do and yadda yadda yadda.

…Yup, Mondays can be hard. Having no more coffee in your mug when you've gotten four hours of sleep is hard. Deciding between two job prospects is hard. Breaking up with a significant other is hard. Hard decisions are HARD! Here's the thing: life is hard. No one ever said it would be easy, clear cut, or universally justifiable one way or the other—they just said it would be worth it. Now I don't know who "they" is, but I think they were onto something with the whole "it'll be worth it" thing.

Growing is worth it.

When you've got a hard decision in front of you with two clear(ish) paths, you know you're supposed to spread your wings and choose the road less traveled. That's typically the "hard" road. The high road.

You know what? Wayne must be one of "them" because there might be clearer ways to think about hard decisions than we often think. It always seems like there are a million different possible outcomes to consider, a thousand paths to choose between, a hundred potential repercussions of our choices that need to be thought about before acting.

But it doesn't have to be so difficult or complicated.

I'm going to hop on the bandwagon and give you two clear-cut justifications for whichever choice you're about to make in life, whether it's a workout class to join (or quit), a hard conversation to have (or not), a bad relationship you know you need to end, or your third attempt at making a chocolate soufflé because those things are seriously difficult and require some encouragement to master.

It's either an opportunity to grow, or an obstacle to keep you from growing.

Simple. As. That. Taking some inspo from my blog name, Coming Up Roses. Bear with me for a hot sec. We're all like roses, in a way. Beautiful, but not without our thorns. Perfectly imperfect, temporary beings. We want to blossom. Our whole life, sometimes, we're on this quest to just keep growing, keep blossoming—learn more, see more, do more, be more. Sometimes we get there, and for a brief moment, we're this picture perfect being. Then it ends, as all things good and bad do, and we eventually die—not to be ridiculously morbid on your Monday or anything. It's true though: in the end, we die. So until then, we have two choices: we can view every hard thing before us as an opportunity to grow, or as an obstacle to keep us from growing. What's it gonna be?

"It's either an opportunity to grow, or an obstacle to keep you from growing."

#CAFFEINATEYOURSOUL

MY ATTITUDE IS GRATITUDE

MY ATTITUDE IS GRATITUDE

A 2011 scientific study said that writing in a gratitude journal before bed helps you sleep better and longer. A 2012 scientific study found that grateful people experience fewer aches and pains and reportedly feel healthier than other people. A 2014 study found that showing appreciation can help you win more friends; thanking a new acquaintance makes them more likely to want an ongoing relationship with you. Another 2014 study determined that gratitude boosts your own self-esteem while lessening your likelihood to fall into the comparison trap. Psychologists have a FIELD DAY with gratitude. It's like this crazy awesome drug that works all sort of magic on our mood, our health, our relationships—the whole nine yards. Also, it's F-R-E-E. Y'all, I'm surprised Harry Potter didn't have a gratitudinous maximus spell to uplift all of Hogwarts.

Since there's absolutely no denying how powerful gratitude is, why isn't everyone and their mother walking around in thanksgiving? I mean, you'd think we'd found the lost ark with the insane psychological hype around simply being grateful.

So why does the world still feel so dang dreary so often?

Because we live in a selfish society. Sometimes, we're just totally caught up.

We feel entitled. We look around expecting someone else to be the answer to our problems, instead of buckling up our work boots and doing the damn thing ourselves. Or, we look around and feel attacked by the universe, or by God Himself, and succumb to a woe-is-me pity party of one. We look at hardships happening, and say, "Why is this happening to me?"

We need an attitude adjustment.

So many authors, coaches, motivational speakers, and their mothers have penned some variation of this pithy one-liner over the years that it's nearly impossible to find the original source (maybe Tony Robbins?):

"What if life isn't happening TO you, but FOR you?"

Tyler Perry once said in an interview, "The trials we go through and the blessings we receive are the same thing. Those trials are lessons you can learn from, and those learnings are blessings."

Isn't that something to chew on with your Cheerios this morning?

It's all happening FOR you, in one way or another. You have NO IDEA what goodness is in store for you—just that He works all things together for good (Romans 8:28). Maybe you need to be stronger. Maybe you need more patience. Maybe you need compassion.

So He's giving you opportunities to be strong, to build strength.

He's giving you opportunities to be patient, to develop patience.

He's giving you opportunities to be compassionate, to foster compassion.

My attitude is gratitude, for the opportunities to grow into my best self. To become who I am destined to be. It's all an opportunity to grow, because growth doesn't come from the easy times. Jim Carrey gave a commencement speech for the Maharishi University of Management's class of 2014 where he said, "When I say life doesn't happen to you, it happens for you, I really don't know if that's true. I'm just making a conscious choice to perceive challenges as something beneficial so that I can deal with them in the most productive way."

Your attitude is a choice. It really is. There are people who have been through absolute GARBAGE in life and still approach every day with newfound hope or happiness. I'm not going to get up on a soapbox and say that you can just choose to be happy over things like clinical depression. But I will say that I think your chosen, adopted attitude 100 percent impacts whatever else is going on in your brain.

Sure, choosing gratitude might not solve all of your problems, but letting misery sink in and fester won't solve 'em, either.

Let your attitude be gratitude. FORCE an attitude of gratitude, and let gratefulness of today make for a better tomorrow.

"Sure, choosing gratitude might not solve all of your problems, but letting misery sink in and fester won't solve 'em, either."

#CAFFEINATEYOURSOUL

I am
BIGGER
than any
excuse

I AM BIGGER THAN ANY EXCUSE

Ask me to do the dishes and I'll find 32 reasons why I can't.

I mean, I can...but I can't. Why?

Because I hate doing the dishes.

I hate the feeling of half-eaten food, and I hate knowing that at any moment, some unidentified mush might land on my hand. The only time you'll find me willingly at the sink is if I'm trying to score points with my husband, or if I'm upset about something because crying into dirty pots and pans somehow feels right. Ha! Call me a crappy wife, call me a wussy, but I SAID IT: not a dishes girl. I'll make up every excuse under the sun why I just can't do dishes. I'm too busy! We have a dishwasher! Let's just use paper plates tonight! We make up excuses when we strongly dislike something, sure, but why do we make up excuses for things that we actually like? Or worse, things that we actually WANT?

There's an old adage that says, "Excuses are nothing more than a reason to fail." The second you give an excuse, you're giving yourself an out. You're making failure an option. You're invalidating yourself and putting on brakes before you've even gotten out of the gate. My guess is that the LAST thing you want to be doing is accidentally or subconsciously halting any progress before you've even had a fighting chance at success. You need to be bigger than any excuse. You ARE bigger than any excuse.

I am bigger than any excuse.

You WANT to build a successful business? That's awesome. You go, girl! But you've got a pocketful of excuses as to why you just can't build a successful business.

I've never done this before! I don't know how to make a budget! I'm not very good at marketing!

Never done this before? Everyone who has ever had a business was once able to say, "I've never done this before." Guess what? Then they did it, and now that isn't an issue anymore.

Don't know how to make a budget? Google, my friend: 1.3 billion answers in 0.61 seconds, right at your fingertips.

Not very good at marketing? Back it up a step. Why do you like your business? Write that down. Why do you think other people should like your business? Write that down. Therein lies a pretty darn good starting spot, in genuinely sharing with folks what is so dang GREAT about what you do. Do you make jewelry and donate proceeds to local women's shelters? Are you helping other entrepreneurs succeed with your affordable accounting services? Did you create a line of shade-inclusive foundations, so that every single woman on the planet has a match? A good business helps provide a solution for a problem. If you're doing that, that's a great building block right there to share it and create conversation (i.e., marketing).

So. . .tell me again about your excuse?

I am bigger than any excuse.

Do you want it more than you're scared of or intimidated by it? The second you find an excuse that's bigger than your why, you've lost that game. Sometimes that's okay if your why isn't all that compelling in the first place. If you're okay with it never happening, then it's okay to make an excuse and cross it off the list permanently. But... are you really okay with it never happening? If in your gut you know you need to make it happen or get it done for your own sake or for someone else's, then it's time to get real with yourself and cut the crap. Really—cut the crap! Stop road blocking your own path. Find a why that is bigger and better than any excuse that might come rolling on up.

Maybe your faith is your why. Maybe your kids or your mom or your third cousin twice removed is your why. Maybe YOU are your why. Whatever your why, it needs to be bigger than any excuse that you, or anyone else, can throw at it.

You are bigger, you are better, and you can.

I can.

I can, I can, I can.

I can go farther. I can go faster. I can

dream bigger. I can believe in myself, really and truly.

I can do more. I can be more. I can love more. I can live more.

I can.

You can make up a thousand reasons why you can't, or you can make up a thousand reasons why you can. It's up to you.

create
your
own joy

CREATE YOUR OWN JOY

On November 25th, I was "mom shamed" for the first time.

I posted a picture on my Instagram that was sponsored by a car company. I was holding my Starbucks out the window, celebrating fall adventures including visiting our month-ish old daughter in the NICU, where she had been since her premature birth on October 17th.

A comment on the post read, "I just don't understand how you can be so happy and make all these posts with your child in the NICU. Any time my kids were in the hospital I never left their side. Are you okay?"

…I know.

SO many folks so kindly and professionally jumped into supportive mode, exactly like any good girlfriend would, and for that I was SO thankful. This Monday Mantra is not to rehash any of that absurdity if being questioned for being "so happy." This Mantra is about JOY. Because later on in that same comment thread, Negative Nancy commented again to say that "the overwhelming joy in each post is disturbing," referring to the joy that I apparently exude through my content.

Girlfriend, the world can be a rough, tough place sometimes. Oftentimes. So I'm here to tell you to create your own joy. Create your own joy.

Create your own opportunities to become more joyful in life. Stop waiting for joy to fall into your lap. I heard the coolest quote on happiness once that said, "Happiness isn't served to you; it's earned. It's created." Think about that.

Happiness is earned. Joy is EARNED.

Meaning, it takes intentional action to achieve.

Happiness isn't just something we magically stumble upon on the sidewalk. Joy isn't something we luckily sit next to on the subway. Sure, we might witness someone ELSE'S joy by sheer happenstance, but to absorb that and carry it onward for ourselves? That takes some effort. It can be HARD to find joy in some circumstances. Heck, maybe even downright impossible. But nothing is impossible with God. And the only way that we've gotten through what we had up to that point was through the sheer power of prayer, and by intentionally choosing to create our own joy every single day—to recognize and celebrate the good things and little victories instead of dwelling on anything less.

Create your own joy.

When you want to become smarter in something, what do you do? You study.

What about becoming stronger? Whether that's at the gym, or in the mind? You practice.

You take control of the one thing that you always can control no matter the circumstance: your perspective. When you put your perspective in check, the pieces start coming together to form a better, brighter picture that more closely resembles your end goal. When you study to become smarter, you're setting yourself up for success by doing everything in your power to know more tomorrow than you do today. Same when you're working out—you do 10 push-ups today so that you can do 15 push-ups tomorrow. Do more today to be more tomorrow.

So you wanna feel more joy in life? What are you doing today to be more joyful tomorrow? Are you filling your moments with things that make you happy? Are you focusing your mind on positives instead of negatives? Are you shifting your perspective to the good instead of harboring on the not so good? If we sit and sulk, we can't blame anyone but ourselves for our lack of happiness. Heck, if anything, we made our own moods MORE sucky by sulking and sitting in that feeling of "everything sucks" rather than TRYING to brighten the day with something sunnier.

Create your own joy.

Here's the real deal. Yes, our situation—in many ways—"sucked."

It sucked having our daughter nearly two whole months early because of unexpected medical complications that put both her and my own life in danger.

It sucked being on magnesium sulfate, and it sucked being catheterized in the vagina. (Yup, that happened.)

It sucked living at the NICU for months, feeling helpless as I worked by her bedside as she slept, just to distract my mind.

It sucked even more when she got mysteriously sick and required an immediate emergency transfer to a bigger, better NICU…an hour and half away from our house.

It sucked commuting every single day to see her instead of snuggling her by the Christmas tree whenever for as long as we want (and it sucked having her first Halloween, Thanksgiving, AND Christmas in the hospital).

It sucked having to watch her from a camera in the moments when we couldn't be physically with her during the day.

BUT. There's a WHOLE LOTTA LIFE to live, and a whole lotta life that can feel pretty darn sucky at times. Every coin has a head AND a tail. Some things in life are obviously joyful. Like being personally serenaded by Justin Timberlake or winning a prize in Bingo (hollah!). Other things in life might not be just joyful—finding the joy in the moment can be like finding a $20 bill in a pocket when you're up to your elbows in dirty clothes on laundry day.

Joy comes from perspective. While there was so much "suck" in the situation, there was still JOY to be found and celebrated in the peanut that is Olivia Grace, who just so happens to be the best thing on planet Earth. (Even though we had NO idea when she would pull through and be discharged from the hospital). Sure, to someone who refuses to choose joy and/or can't create her own, being joyful in our current situation might seem absurd—downright delusional. But at the end of that day, I feel sorry for folks like that. Because when you can't create your own joy, your life lacks a whole 'nother level of happiness that no one is responsible for but yourself. Girlfriend, it's time to stop b*tching about your own life if you're not actively working to change it.

Of course, some things like mental illness or a lack of privilege pose legitimate roadblocks on the journey towards a joy-filled best self. This isn't to ignore that—it's to simply hold yourself responsible for as much as you reasonably and realistically can, in creating joy within the context of your own everyday life.

We all have "those days."

Those days where you just feel like you're being pulled in seven different directions too many, and you're on the brink of either doing something awesome or falling hard.

Those days where you can't decide whether you're really, really excited and on top of it or really, really scared and three steps behind the pack.

Those days when you just wish you had a personal assistant that could keep track of life for you and pass you Fudge Shoppe cookies and force you to hit the gym afterwards and then take over for the night while you kick back with some champagne.

Here's the thing: those days will come.

The days of feeling insecure, stretched too thin, uncertain, and scared don't add up to a bad life or a bad person or a bad business or a bad anything.

They're just those days.

In the end, there's one key to make it through those days: create your own joy. Don't just take it from me—take it from good ol' Albus Dumbledore. "Happiness can be found in the darkest of times, if only one remembers to turn on the light."

Create your own joy.

"Take control of the one thing that you always can control no matter the circumstance: your perspective. When you put your perspective in check, the pieces start coming together to form a better, brighter picture that more closely resembles your end goal."

#CAFFEINATEYOURSOUL

WORK HARD AND BE KIND

Kevin Durant said it best: "Hard work beats talent when talent doesn't work hard." No matter where you started, you've got what it takes to finish—and finish first, at that. Like the tortoise and the hare, it ain't over 'til it's over, and working hard at your own pace can be the golden ticket to success at the finish line. But in the end, it's not JUST about working hard. If you work hard, but you're an asshat, you'll leave a sour taste in everyone's mouth. There's one ultimate combo that's a winner winner chicken dinner every time: Work hard and be kind.

First off: Hard work. It's really freaking important. "If it's important to you, you'll find a way. If it's not, you'll find an excuse." I'd say it should seem like a no-brainer, but it continues to baffle me how often I see folks complain about where they're at in life (or where they're not), with an expectation for others to fix the problem for them. Of course we can't inherently do it all or fix it all ourselves—again, not Wonder Woman—but we can often surprise ourselves with just how dang much we ARE capable of without even knowing it.

It's important to define what hard work means to you, too. Nancy Next Door's definition of "hard work" might be different than yours, and you know why? Nancy Next Door's entire upbringing, experiences, and LIFE are different than yours, and that's A-okay. You've gotta put in the elbow grease. We live in a world today that forgets elbow grease exists unless Google tells us it does. Everything is searchable in half a millisecond, and there's not necessarily a push to think when we're in a pinch. Instead, we ask Siri for answers and let a computer do the hard work for us.

But we're still humans. Everything can be digitized, but not everything is better digitized. Hard work and elbow grease still go a long way. Good communication (in person/offline) still goes a long way. Unless we wanna become vegetables that do whatever a hardware system of algorithms tells us to do, we've gotta keep on keepin' on, working hard to find our own answers and pave our own paths.

Working hard matters.

Second: Be kind. Being "kind" is better than being "nice." Nice by definition means pleasant, agreeable, satisfactory, or fine. Being agreeable to all isn't necessarily a good thing! You won't be everyone's cup of tea, and that's how it should be. But what you SHOULD be is intentionally kind to those whose paths cross yours. Smile at the old man in the grocery store, and let him in front of you in line if he has less in her cart. Exercise patience on the phone when scheduling appointments—it'll rub off on the secretaries handling books, and impact everyone they speak to that day. Be truly open and loving to people you meet, no matter their background, gender, race, job title, skin color. The world would be better if every single person on it was intentionally kind to every single other person— point blank period. No quips or qualms about it. If everyone's hearts were changed and came from a place of love and understanding instead of irrational judgment or pointed hatred, we could raise different, better generations. You don't need a reason to be nice to someone other than they are another human being. They deserve kindness just as much as you do. Being kind matters.

May it serve as your golden rule this week and then some: Work hard and be kind.

"You don't need a reason to be nice to someone other than they are another human being. They deserve kindness just as much as you do. Being kind Matters."

#CAFFEINATEYOURSOUL

I WILL BE A LIGHT

One of my all-time favorite quotes is from a woman named Edith Wharton. It goes a little something like this. "There are two ways of spreading light: to be the candle, or the mirror that reflects it."

While it's SO GOOD to always spread others' light, I know some of you reading these words are the most selfless women on the planet. You'd put other folks before yourselves without second thought. So I don't want you to forget about your OWN light while you're busy mirroring theirs.

Because in doing so, we risk forgetting we have a light of our own altogether.

Promise me something? This week, you will be a light. "I will be a light."

How often do we go through day-to-day life not even realizing our potential? Half the time, we can't even comprehend what we're truly capable of, because we either 1) haven't been in a situation where it's been required of us to test it, or 2) haven't gone out on that ledge to make it happen. We

don't necessarily live every day as if it's our last because we're not always attuned to the finite nature of life; we're human, and we forget that sometimes. We get burnt out and hungry and overwhelmed, and we turn off the real world and turn on Netflix to forget life for a hot sec. Then we hit replay tomorrow.

We're not always turned on to our own potential.

So, we don't always shine at our brightest, or anywhere close to our brightest.

Beyond that, we get scared. We get scared of everything that would/could/should happen if we're operating at 100 percent in a judgmental, jaded world. You figure that someone somewhere will be offended, hurt, or otherwise bitter about your success and your shine. Eventually, you'd rather not shine so bright—or worse, not shine at all—to save face with them or prevent any tensions down the road (even though any tensions would be entirely rooted in THEIR own insecurity and self-doubts).

OY. It's exhausting! Let's make it easy:

Give yourself permission to shine your brightest. No matter the circumstance, no matter the company.

I know, I know…"Shine your light! Never let anyone dull your sparkle!" These are overused, cliché phrases that sometimes fail to pack a punch since they're plastered on every cheesy Hallmark card or board-walk souvenir. So let's think of a visual here, since I'm one of those visual learners who's all about a good pie chart or stick-figure diagram.

The sun shines each and every day, without a doubt. It's going to be there and it's going to be bright, regardless of what's happening or who's watching. How often do we hold ourselves back, or cower away from our own lights, in fear of how it will be received by others? We worry about being judged or misunderstood, and we let others' reception and perception of us shift how we present ourselves to the world. The sun is KNOWN for being the brightest, hottest, fiercest ball of badass fire in the sky. I'm sure the cavepeople were a bit taken aback at first—Fire? In the sky? Throw water at it! IT CAN'T BE!—but once they figured out that sun was going to shine regardless of who they were or what they did, they figured they might as well get used to it and use it for good.

Similarly, if people were to know YOU for your best self…dontcha think they could better utilize you for all of YOUR good, too?

"I will be a light."

When the sun eclipses, it's a nice illustrator for what happens when the seemingly untouchable become somewhat, kinda sorta touchable-ish. Everyone wants a piece of it.

The sun is in this more vulnerable state, with its light being hidden by the moon, and all God's green earth freaks the freak out, because this is such a rare thing. Grab yo' glasses! Grab yo' telescopes! We're headed to Wyoming to eclipse watch! Everyone and their mom is eagerly anticipating the few minutes to behold something so impossible to behold. In those brief moments of total eclipse (of the heart…had to), the brightest beacon of light in our everyday sky (heck, the ONLY beacon of light) is darkened.

That doesn't mean it stops shining.

That doesn't mean it's being overcome or "losing" at all.

That doesn't mean it lasts.

It is still doin' it's thaaaang, being a light and shining regardless of what's covering it in that one moment in time.

Similarly, sometimes in life, people want to take advantage of your dark spots. These people are asshats. They are the ones who find joy in assuming that you have been reduced somehow, and that you have been lowered to their level and are now within their grasp. These people are very much mistaken. A momentary vulnerability does nothing to lessen your worth. It doesn't make you flawed, and it doesn't necessarily mean it was even your doing in the first place. The same way that the sun continues to shine and be a light no matter what's covering it, so too should we refuse to let societal standards or everyday happenstance diminish our lights.

"I will be a light."

Light only gets brighter by being shared. This is even more so important to remember in the world today—a world so torn by hatred, judgment, and misunderstanding. We need lights. We need beacons of light to shine as examples of goodness—of kindness.

We need you.

"I will be a light."

Being a light doesn't mean you're shining at others' expense.

Light only gets brighter by being shared. Another popular gem: "Thousands of candles can be lit from a single candle, and the life of the candle will not be shortened." The best way to start a fire is to start it yourself, both in your own life and in the lives of the people around you. From there, if we all continue to be lights—to shine fully and strongly—we can hope to spark a fire unquenchable by any societal eclipses.

We can (and should) be lights through

any darkness. Light is not the absence of dark. Rather, darkness is the absence of light. Light ALWAYS overcomes dark. Just as the sun will bounce right back to shining moments after being seemingly overcome by darkness, so too can you be a source of light and inspiration for anyone and everyone in your path. Heck, you might even light them up, too.

The light shines in the darkness, and the darkness has not overcome it. (John 1:5)

For we are God's masterpiece. He has created us anew in Christ Jesus, so we can do the good things He planned for us long ago. (Ephesians 2:10)

"Light only gets brighter by being shared. This is even more so important to remember in the world today—a world so torn by hatred, judgment, and misunderstanding. We need lights. We need beacons of light to shine as examples of goodness—of kindness. We need you."

#CAFFEINATEYOURSOUL

Faith it 'til you Make it

FAITH IT 'TIL YOU MAKE IT

I'm a big fan of "fake it 'til you make it," but sometimes faking it until you make it doesn't quite cut it. Sometimes, you need something more—something bigger.

Faith.

Whether or not you consider yourself to be a particularly spiritual or religious person, this mantra has two sides to the story. Enter: Faith it 'til you make it.

Sure, there's something to be said for playing the part of your dream self until that dream self becomes your everyday reality. "Faking" it isn't really faking anymore. Many people swear by it—it gets you in the game, ready to step up to center stage like an understudy taking on the lead role on show night.

But sometimes, faking it just ain't gonna cut it.

You need something to believe in so strongly that you just know that you're going to get through the other side—a side of "I made it!" that feels oh so good. You need something to call your rock, so that in times of stress, hardship, or doubt, you can remain grounded in your truth.

For me (and for maybe you, too?), my truth and my rock is Christ. So "faith it 'til you make it" resonates, because I wholeheartedly believe that I can rely on divine help to inspire my thoughts and direction, and to help point me to where I need to go to achieve not only what I want, but what He wants. We're taught through Scripture that God is not going to lead us astray. He has a uniquely intricate plan set out for each of us, and it's ours to discern through prayer and practice. It's our choice to tune into that plan and live by it, but it's also our calling. When we have that faith and act on it, I think God gives us a little booster. He looks down on us with favor, in all of our human flaws and human error, and He just wraps us in love and guidance and direction to help us get to where we want and need to go.

Besides helping to make things happen, "faith it 'til you make it" is that thing to repeat to yourself in the mirror when you're this close to giving up. When times are hard—really hard—and all you want to do is throw in the towel, sometimes the only thing that helps me get by is faith that I'm here for a reason, and that things are going to be okay. You know what else?

…Things are going to be okay for you, too.

Have FAITH that your purpose is strong and you are here for a reason. Keep the faith, even when it's hard because it's freakin' hard to not know all the answers. It's hard to lose that sense of control over our lives, especially when we think we're just in boss mode of our own accord. It's hard to surrender that and just have it be in God's hands. Sometimes, I just want to hop up to heaven and say, "God, I need this, like, yesterday. Can you make this happen? At this time? With these people?" I mean, that would be nice. But that control isn't the purpose of faith.

Faith it 'til you make it.

Because sometimes, you have no clue what's ahead. You can't see the path, you aren't sure of next steps, and you're nervous about choosing the wrong option or making the wrong call. Enter faith. You have faith that God will guide you towards where you're meant to be, because He's lookin' out. He always does. Keep the faith.

Of course, I get that not everyone agrees with me—that not everyone is a Christian or believes in this divine plan in life. For you, this mantra still applies.

Faith doesn't have to be in a higher power all the time; faith can also be in yourself.

Have faith that you'll get there.

Have faith that you've got the smarts, the drive, the resources, the connections, the talent, and the capabilities to make it happen—to make it to where you so desperately want to go, and where you know you CAN go.

Have faith that you're doing what you can at this very moment to advance, and if you're not, have faith that you'll soon recognize that and be equipped with what you need to readjust course at that point and move forward again toward your goals.

Have faith that you are prepared to perform.

And just keep faithin' it 'til you make it.

GIVE UP
GUILT

We hear all the time that shaming is bad. Body shaming yourself or others—shaming anyone for something, really—isn't exactly encouraged practice. Shame is this intense feeling that you yourself are bad; most of us could probably agree (or should!) that we cannot under any circumstances place that sort of shadow on someone's beautiful life. But guilt.

Oh, guilt.

Guilt is that momentary shame over a specific action or happening that ends with you feeling bad about yourself or your choices. ("I am bad" = shame, while "I did something bad" = guilt). It's a feeling knocked outta the park by society. Because it's socially acceptable (and sometimes, encouraged!) to feel guilty after eating cake or pizza, or for choosing to binge watch Netflix instead of launching a business or changing the world. We're made to feel guilty for times when we're not on the "hustle," and made to feel like the hustlers' road is the only road that heads for Success City. We're made to feel guilty when we take a hot second to REST and put our own self-love and self-care over cranking out more work.

We're made to feel guilty.

This changes today. We need to give up guilt.

We need to give up guilt, because sometimes, we owe the little things to ourselves. Give up guilt that you bought the shoes or ate a second piece of cake. Give up guilt that you just spent three hours of your night watching The Bachelor and the after special instead of cranking through emails. Give up guilt that you didn't volunteer to bake three dozen cupcakes for the bake sale or chair the community outreach committee, or that you didn't help your friend move cross-country.

Give up guilt.

There's a difference between too much and just enough, but sometimes that line is just so blurred that you find yourself basing decisions almost entirely on in-the-moment feelings and circumstances. You "don't feel like" working more, so you turn to NCIS reruns. You "don't feel like" doing laundry, so you let your dirty clothes hang out while you paint your nails and bake cookies. Then, you EAT the cookies, too!

But we've gotta give up the guilt. Otherwise, we forget how to rest. We forget how to let ourselves go for a moment or enjoy the little things, because we become afraid of the little things. We end up letting small joys trump our peace, because we've got this sense of guilt that creeps up all over the place and leaves a nasty scar.

Give up guilt. Be okay with your humanity. If you made a mistake—an actual, true mistake—own it, apologize for it, and make amends to it. Then, let go of the guilt, because it just gets heavier if you keep carrying it around with you.

It would be totally silly to say "give up guilt!" and just do whatever the heck we want, whenever, as a result. That wouldn't be productive, healthy, or sane, really, but that's not the point here. The point is, you've got smarts. If you've made it this far, you probably know the difference in your gut between right and wrong, or "too much" and "just enough." We're not saying live recklessly, folks. We're saying give up the guilt from those occasional carefree moments. Guilt tripping because you allowed yourself a good time or a bit of self-indulgence is negative, useless, and ultimately, self-destructive.

If we're not careful, repeated guilt can start to feel like shame, and shame is a heavy burden to bear. Feeling guilty over our rest or small respites from life is the quickest route to unhappiness, discontent, and burn out.

You know the saying "everything in moderation?" If you're having a second piece of cake every single night for three weeks straight, it might be time to reconsider your choices for the sake of your arteries. If you're online shopping every night and burning through plastic, it might be time to think twice before hitting "buy" for the sake of your credit score. Maintaining moderation and being smart about choices is always going to be a good theory to go through life, but this should never ever (ever) come at the expense of how you feel about yourself.

You're human.

You're going to have the urge to break Whole 30 or whatever other "diet" or eating regimen you're following, and sometimes, you might give in to that urge and grab a chocolate chip cookie. Of course, it's not ideal to break a promise to yourself. It's even worse if you then turn to then hating and shaming yourself and feeling guilty all day for having the cookie. It keeps building, and you're setting your brain up for one helluvah battle. If you decide to splurge on something—anything—just do the damn thing and enjoy every second.

Do it, savor it, soak it all up, and then decide your next step from there. You can get back on track.

Life's too short. Give up guilt.

I am what I
what I
BECOME

I AM WHAT I BECOME

You know how you are what you eat? Not sure how true that is, because I'm yet to turn into Trader Joe's Unexpected Cheddar Cheese and a glass of Cabernet. So I've got one to top it:

You are what you become.

I am what I become.

Raise your hand if you know that something from your past is currently impacting something in your present, or your thought process about your future. Maybe you don't know—maybe you have NO IDEA—so raise your hand if you *think* there's something there that *might* be impacting your present or future. If we were hanging out in person, I've got a feeling I'd be looking at a room of raised hands. You've got some *baggage*, sister, and it might not even feel like baggage. Some of our baggage might feel like running to a gate, solo, with three packed suitcases in tow through Chicago's O'Hare International airport (so, a nightmare in which I almost blacked out—true

story). Some of our baggage might feel like a light carry-on, or even a little crossbody bag. No matter your story, I'd bet you've got something you're carrying.

Maybe it's the backlash from being bullied as a kid.

Maybe it's the loss of a loved one.

Maybe it's the pain of seeing a friend battle an addiction.

Maybe it's the feeling that you'll never be truly known, or truly loved.

Girlfriend, no matter the size, that baggage is *heavy*. This week, I want to encourage you to lighten your load a bit because even if you didn't realize it at the time, you've been carrying a weight from your past around on your back that's impacting how you show up in your life today.

Sister, your past does not define your future. It might have defined it up to this point, and you might've thought it would define your future forevermore, but it doesn't have to. It really doesn't.

Your past does not define your NOW, either.

You are what you become. *I am what I become.* In the world of manifesting or visualization, it's common practice to really envision what you want to happen—really *see* it in detail—with a goal of bringing it into fruition. I think it's important to incorporate the Big Man Upstairs here though, too, since no amount of manifestation can change the plan that He has written in stone for our lives.

You are what God intends you to be, and you will be what God intends you to become, so long as you get the heck out of your own way.

Your past does not define you; what you do today defines you. How you choose to overcome defines you. We become what we think about, and we become like the five people we surround ourselves with most. That's why visualizing or "manifesting" positively impacts your life; focusing on a specific vision or thought for your future plans it into your subconscious, altering all of your actions from that point forward to position you towards success. Want to run a marathon? See yourself crossing that finish line. Close your eyes and feel the runner number pinned to your shirt. Feel the sweat on your forehead and the pain in your legs. When you can so clearly envision yourself doing or being something, it makes perfect sense for you to tie up your Nikes and hit the gym, because you've nearly convinced yourself that *you are a runner.*

I am what I become.

You become like the five people you surround yourself with most. Surround yourself with Negative Nancies who complain constantly? Soon, you might start complaining more yourself. You've become a complainer. You ARE a complainer. Because you are what you become. Similarly, surround yourself with optimistic go-getters, and you might find yourself waking up at 5 a.m. like them to become more diligent with your morning routine, or to become more grateful through gratitude journaling. You ARE grateful, because you are what you become.

That hard sh*t in your past? You can get through that, too. You are not that person anymore; you are stronger, grittier, better. It might take more than closing your eyes and visualizing something different, but dang it, you are not that! You are what you become next.

Your future is formed by your next step, not your last one.

TODAY I COMMIT

TODAY I COMMIT

You've done it—you've gotten through the other 51 Mondays of the year. Pat yourself on the back and pop the bubbly, would ya? Because it's never too early to celebrate new beginnings, and with a New Year right around the corner, I'd say champagne feels just right.

Today's the day. What day?

Today is the day you commit. Now, hopefully you made a commitment way back when, about 51 Mondays ago, but just in case it took you a bit longer to catch on, no problemo. We're here today to commit together (because accountability buddies are a glorious thing).

Some folks are S-C-A-R-E-D of commitment—are you one of 'em? They won't stick around in relationships, won't try something new in fear of actually liking it too much, won't make plans just in case something better comes up. Since I don't have enough space in my word count left to convince you why you should nix the

fear of commitment altogether, I'll leave you with this:

Be willing to honestly recognize the big dreams on your heart and the purpose on your soul, and commit to making the necessary changes to make it happen.

Your life will change the second you start actively changing it. And "IT" is up for definition: your relationships, your job, your body, your mindset. Commit to the change—commit to making it happen.

Commit to yourself. Commit to everyone in your life who is counting on you, and commit to your best self because SHE is counting on you, too.

Today I commit to getting uncomfortable for the sake of growth.

Today I commit to keeping the promises I've made to myself.

Today I commit to cutting the noise and saying no when it's the necessary answer.

Today I commit to embracing the balancing act of life, and giving myself grace.

Today I commit to stepping out of my comfort zone and doing hard things.

Today I commit to an attitude of gratitude and a willingness to light up my own life, and the lives of those I love.

Today I commit to becoming my very best self, because that is what I am meant to be and deserve to be.

Do you commit, too?

CHECK-IN!

1. What's an excuse that you've been clinging to that might be holding you back in life?

2. Where can you get a little uncomfortable to grow in that area?

3. What are you putting out into the world, from your attitude to your actions? Is there any space or area that needs more kindness, more light, more service, more discipline?

ABOUT THE AUTHOR

Erica Gwynn is an author, podcaster, teacher, speaker, and successful lifestyle influencer. She's the founder of Coming Up Roses, an online community rooted in the belief that while not everything in life is pretty and every rose has its thorn, we can still live in full bloom with a positive perspective where everything is coming up roses. (We also believe in affordable fashion, dry shampoo, laughing at yourself, and frequent wine-and-cheese nights).

Her online course, BossPitch, was born in 2016 after Erica successfully made her "little online blog" her full-time, six-figure job and knew she had to teach other aspiring bloggers how to do the same. She has gone on to teach hundreds of students how to know their worth and charge accordingly, in pitching and politely persisting their way to dream brand partnerships.

Her podcast, THRIVE, has practical tips and weekly interviews to bring listeners from a life of simply surviving, to thriving.

She has a Bachelor of Science in Economics with concentrations in Marketing and Management from the Wharton School at UPenn and is certified in Spanish, but she definitely couldn't tell you a single thing from Corporate Finance class (she was too busy blogging, but hey—it worked out).

Erica is based right outside Philadelphia with her husband Jamie, their miracle daughter, Olivia Grace, and their rescue cat, Purrcy.

You can find Erica online at cominguprosestheblog.com.

 @ericaligenza

 @cominguprosestheblog

 @msericaligenza